The
INTERMISSION
of
GRACE

BIBLICAL ADVANCED BASICS
book two

The

INTERMISSION

of

GRACE

Jesus Christ died for your sins, was buried,
and He rose again the third day

FREDERICK E. LEWIS

RELIANT
PUBLISHING
A DIVISION OF REDEMPTION PRESS

Published by Reliant Publishing, an imprint of Redemption Press, PO Box 427, Enumclaw, WA 98022.

Toll-Free (844) 2REDEEM (273-3336)

Redemption Press is honored to present this title in partnership with the author. The views expressed or implied in this work are those of the author. Redemption Press provides our imprint seal representing design excellence, creative content, and high-quality production.

Unless otherwise noted, all Scripture quotations are taken from the Holy Bible, King James Version, Cambridge, 1769.

Scriptures marked (ERV) are from the English Revised Version. Copyright © 1885 by University of Cambridge.

Scriptures marked (NKJV) are from the New King James Version®. Copyright © 1982 by Thomas Nelson. Used by permission. All rights reserved.

Scriptures marked (EGTR) are from the Erasmus' Greek Textus Receptus, 1516, are in public domain.

Scriptures marked (GM) are from the Greek Majority Text, 1982, fall under fair-use guidelines. Sourced from the Online Bible software program.

Scriptures marked (MTB) are from the Majority Text Byzantine, 1991 fall under fair-use guidelines. Sourced from the Online Bible software program.

Scriptures marked (GWH) are from the Greek Wescott Hort Text, 1881, public domain.

Scriptures marked (GB) are from the Geneva Bible, 1599, public domain.

Scriptures marked (Wycliffe) are from the John Wycliffe Bible, 1384, public domain.

Scriptures marked (Purvey) are from the John Purvey Bible, 1395, public domain.

Scriptures marked (LV) are from the Latin Vulgate, public domain.

ISBN 13: 978-1-64645-371-9 (Paperback)
978-1-64645-373-3 (ePub)
978-1-64645-372-6 (Mobi)

Library of Congress Catalog Card Number: 2007908237

Dedication

This book is dedicated to the many Bible teachers I have been exposed to over the years. Their diligent work to bring the truths out of Scripture has made it possible to understand the Bible for anyone who has a desire.

Contents

Introduction

For this book to achieve its maximum effectiveness, it is strongly suggested that you read Book One, *Understanding the Bible and End Times*, by this author first. By doing so, you will have a solid foundation for this book to build upon. Book One took almost thirty years to write, due to all the confusion centered around the many systems of interpretation for the Holy Bible. There are basically two camps: dispensational and covenant. Within each camp, there are many variations of doctrine, depending on how you piece together the various programs used by God to deal with His creation. I believe that today we are in a stand-alone program that began soon after the stoning of Stephen in Acts Chapter 7. If you try to mix in any of God's other programs, you will come up with a confusing mixture, and this explains why we have so many differing systems of Bible interpretation that have accumulated over the years. This book will go into detail about the various programs and why their improper mixing produces confusion.

One thought that gave me energy and sustained my interest, over the 30 years, was that initially I came to believe that God would not have inspired a book to be written that hardly anyone could understand. I realized that I had always believed, from my youth, that someday I would be able to understand the Bible. In I Corinthians 14:33 the apostle Paul was inspired to write, "For God is not the author of confusion, but of peace, as in all churches of the saints." With all the denominational differences in our churches today, would you say that we can observe "confusion"? Well, if God is not the author, who is? Would it be beneath Satan to sow seeds of confusion to frustrate the efforts in our churches to fulfill our commission for today? (For more on today's commission, see Chapter 4.)

Book One concerns an understanding of end times; however, the author believes that in order to understand end times one must be able to understand the Bible, and to be able to understand the Bible, two things must be present. First and foremost, one must have the aid of the Holy Spirit. Therefore, Book One, Part 1 presents the plan of salvation. It is only after we are saved that the Holy Spirit indwells us and can assist with our understanding of the Scriptures. Second, one must apply the principle of right division described in II Timothy 2:15: "Study to shew thyself approved unto God, a workman that needeth not to be ashamed, rightly dividing the word of truth." This will prevent the improper mixing of the two main programs of God and eliminate the confusion that would result.

The entire Bible can be divided into two parts, the two main programs of God. God has an earthly plan and a heavenly plan. This idea is introduced in the first verse of the Bible, Genesis 1:1: "In the beginning God created the heaven and the earth." Then the Bible goes on to describe the plan or program He has for each. The chart at the end of this introduction illustrates which books of the Bible pertain to which program. You will notice that the books of Acts and Hebrews are transitional from one program to the other and back again. These two programs remain delineated throughout the Bible and in the eternal state we find the new heaven and the new earth. The earthly program is often referred to as prophecy and the heavenly program as the mystery. The reason the Bible calls the heavenly program the mystery is that it was kept secret until midway through the book of Acts. Failure to recognize this results in confusion when one tries to understand the Scriptures by improperly combining the two programs. We must "rightly divide" to avoid that confusion.

The heavenly program is the one that is in effect today and the earthly program is on temporary hold until the heavenly program runs its course. Another reason the Bible calls the heavenly plan or program the mystery is that it was not forecast in the prophetic Scriptures. It was a mystery, or secret, hid in God.

"And to make all men see what is the fellowship of the mystery, which from the beginning of the world hath been hid in God, who created all things by Jesus Christ" (Ephesians 3:9).

An important discovery when you implement the principle of right division is that you find that the current church, the body of Christ, began in the mid-part of the book of Acts and not in Acts Chapter 2 on the day of Pentecost. That church was a continuation of the "church in the wilderness" under Moses (Acts 7:38— see Chapter 4).

The earthly program involves the gospel of the kingdom and the heavenly program involves the gospel of the grace of God. God's grace has been displayed in both programs, but we are now in a time of the outpouring of pure grace in what is called "the dispensation of the grace of God" (Ephesians 3:2).

The earthly program began to be interrupted, by the heavenly program at the raising up of the apostle Paul, in Acts Chapter 9. The heavenly program will run until the rapture of the church, the body of Christ. Then, after an indeterminate period of time, the earthly program will resume with seven years of tribulation, where the events described in the book of Revelation, will play out. It is important that we understand today's program to be able to explain it understandably to anyone interested in wanting to know how to be reconciled to God and therefore be delivered from the wrath to come.

"And to wait for his Son from heaven, whom he raised from the dead, even Jesus, which delivered us from the wrath to come" (I Thessalonians 1:10).

There has been much conjecture in theological circles, over the years, on the Scriptural basis for the apostle Paul. Some say he should have been chosen by Peter and the other apostles instead of Matthias. This can be quickly dispelled from the Scriptures in Acts 1:21–26:

> Wherefore of these men which have companied with us all the time that the Lord Jesus went in and out among us, Beginning from the baptism of John, unto that same day that he was taken up from us, must one be ordained to be a witness with us of his resurrection. And they appointed two, Joseph called Barsabas, who was surnamed Justus, and Matthias. And they prayed, and said, Thou, Lord, which knowest the hearts of all men, shew whether of these two thou hast chosen, That he may take part of this ministry and apostleship, from which Judas by transgression fell, that he might go to his own place. And they gave forth their lots; and the lot fell upon Matthias; and he was numbered with the eleven apostles.

Paul did not fill the two requirements to be a candidate. Some say that he was a spare apostle, in case one of the twelve died, and that he preached the same message as the Twelve. In Chapter 5 of this book, the case is made for the fact that there are two gospels: the gospel of the kingdom, preached by the twelve apostles, and the gospel of the grace of God, preached by the apostle Paul.

God chose Paul to go to the Gentiles and Jews alike with the new gospel. This is clear from the three passages in the book of Acts that record his conversion: Acts 9:1–31; 22:6–21; and 26:13–18. During Paul's ministry of approximately 30 years, he tried to go to the Jews as well as the Gentiles. Many of Jews rejected this new gospel as recorded in three passages: Acts 13:46; 18:6; and 28:27–28.

Paul understood from his conversion that his mission was to take the new gospel to primarily the Gentiles. This is brought out in Romans 11:13–14: "For I speak to you Gentiles, inasmuch as I am the apostle of the Gentiles, I magnify mine office: If by any means I may provoke to emulation them which are my flesh, and might save some of them."

If questions arise during your reading, just keep reading as those questions will most likely be addressed and answered as you continue. Note, you will notice reiteration of some phrases and Scripture, for emphasis, that describe different angles on a particular view.

The main goal of this book is to clearly explain exactly what is necessary for someone to be sure they will spend eternity in heaven with God the Father, God the Son, and God the Holy Spirit. A secondary goal is to give readers a key to unlock the Scriptures, for a more enjoyable and informing experience, when reading and studying their Bible.

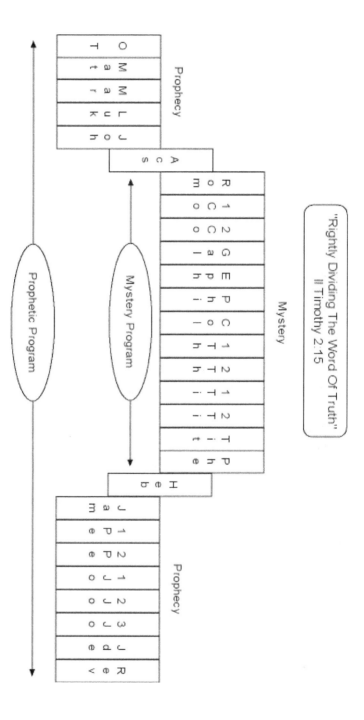

"Rightly Dividing The Word Of Truth"
II Timothy 2:15

Note: The books of Acts and Hebrews are transitional from one program to the other and back again.

©

CHAPTER 1

The Intermission of Grace

This author uncovered a simplifying concept in 1988. This came about as a result of a friend being exposed to a Bible tract titled, "Simple as can Be" by C. R. Stam, written back in the 1940s. This Bible tract's impact is described in detail in the Preface, and reprinted in Part 1, of *Understanding the Bible and End Times* by this author, who had been struggling to understand end times known as *eschatology*, since the mid-1970s. It took another eighteen years, implementing the simplifying concept, for a total of thirty years, to publish the book mentioned above, with confidence, in 2006. Now, after fifteen more years, I offer this Book Two.

It was this simplifying concept that enabled me to discover the "Intermission of Grace." So, let us define our terms. The simplifying concept centers around the fact that God changed His dealings with mankind midway through the book of Acts. At that time, He essentially put the earthly, prophetic program on hold, and began the heavenly, mystery program that we are in currently. By using the principle of right division from II Timothy 2:15, you can separate the two programs. This will avoid the confusion that would result by improperly mixing part of the on-hold prophetic program with the currently running mystery program The Intermission of Grace is this author's way of assigning a term to the current program with which we are all familiar.

If you think of the entire Bible, in a metaphorical sense, as a two-act play, you have Act One as the Old Testament and Old Covenant, followed by Act Two as the New Testament and New Covenant, and of course there will be a Finale when the eternal state begins. There are many scenes in each act that record what God has revealed to us in the Scriptures. The transition from the old to the new was prophesied to be a continuous process, but based on the simplifying concept, God interrupted the process, at the raising up of the apostle Paul, with what this author has identified as the Intermission of Grace. Just as in a modern stage play, nothing in the play transpires during the intermission. Now, during the rest of the Intermission of Grace, nothing will transpire from Act Two in terms of prophecy. Act Two will resume after the intermission has ended and will be discussed and explained as you read the succeeding chapters. Both terms, simplifying concept and Intermission of Grace, are unique, and I do not believe they have ever been used before to help explain the interruption. This book will endeavor to explain, in detail, the ramifications of the interruption and the benefits to the student of Scripture for the recognition of its existence.

Some of the benefits for the believer for recognizing the Intermission of Grace include the following:

1. One can realize that there are no denominations in the Bible and that the many denominational differences are due to improperly mixing parts of both programs. (See II Timothy 2:15.)

2. We are currently in an unprophesied program, called the "mystery, which from the beginning of the world hath been hid in God." (See Ephesians 3:9.)

3. The current program will continue until the "fulness of the Gentiles be come in." (See Romans 11:25 and read Part 4 in this author's book, *Understanding the Bible and End Times.*)

4. The plan of salvation, called the "gospel of the grace of God," has been simplified to be based on pure grace in this "dispensation of the grace of God." (See Acts 20:24; Ephesians 3:2.)

5. One can be instantly and eternally saved ("after ye believed ye were sealed with that Holy Spirit of promise") by believing the gospel that Jesus Christ died for your sins, was buried, and rose again the third day. (See Ephesians 1:13; I Corinthians 15:1–4.)

6. There are no works required for salvation today, but we are "created in Christ Jesus unto good works, which God hath before ordained that we should walk in them." (See Romans 4:5; Ephesians 2:8–10.)

7. There will be a "judgment seat of Christ" where we will gain and/or lose rewards for our works. (See Chapter 7 of this volume.)

8. You are baptized into (or identified with) the body of Christ by the Holy Spirit the moment you believe the gospel. (See I Corinthians 12:13.)

9. There is only "one baptism" (spiritual) during this time. (See Chapter 12 and Ephesians 4:4–5.)

10. We will be "delivered (us) from the wrath to come" in the "day of the Lord" and the "great

tribulation." (See I Thessalonians 1:10; 5:9; Matthew 24:21.)

11. We have a blessed hope in what is known as the rapture, where we will be rescued before God resumes the prophetic program with the revealing of the Antichrist, seven-year tribulation, battle of Armageddon, one thousand-year millennial kingdom reign of Christ on the earth, battle of Gog and Magog, White Throne Judgment, lake of fire, and the eternal state with the new heaven, new earth, and new Jerusalem. (See Titus 2:13; I Thessalonians 4:16–18.)

12. "All things work together for good." (See Chapter 16 of this volume.)

13. The unlocking of the Scriptures, due to the recognition of the Intermission of Grace, should result in a higher enjoyment as well as a deeper understanding of the entire Bible.

The lead-up to the Intermission of Grace begins with the seventy weeks prophecy from Daniel 9:24–27. (See Chapter 13 of this volume.)

> Seventy weeks are determined upon thy people and upon thy holy city, to finish the transgression, and to make an end of sins, and to make reconciliation for iniquity, and to bring in everlasting righteousness, and to seal up the vision and prophecy, and to anoint the most Holy. Know therefore and understand, that from the going forth of the commandment to restore and to build Jerusalem unto the Messiah the Prince shall be seven weeks, and threescore and two weeks: the street shall be built again, and the wall, even in troublous times. And after threescore and two weeks shall Messiah be cut off, but not for himself: and the people of the prince that shall come shall destroy

the city and the sanctuary; and the end thereof shall be with a flood, and unto the end of the war desolations are determined. And he shall confirm the covenant with many for one week: and in the midst of the week he shall cause the sacrifice and the oblation to cease, and for the overspreading of abominations he shall make it desolate, even until the consummation, and that determined shall be poured upon the desolate. (Daniel 9:24–27)

In Chapter 13 of this book titled, *Three Days and Three Nights*, you will learn that seventy weeks represents seventy weeks of years. Seventy times 7 days in a week equals 490 years. Sixty-nine of those weeks, or 483 years (173,880 days) were to elapse "unto the Messiah the Prince." Also, we can determine that the date for the "commandment to restore and to build Jerusalem" was March 14, 445 BC. If you add the 173,880 days, you come up to Sunday, April 6, 32 AD. This is the day, Palm Sunday, Jesus Christ rode into Jerusalem as Messiah—the triumphal entry. Until that day He would rebuke anyone who would refer to Him as Messiah or King. But on that day Scripture records that, when the Pharisees heard the multitude refer to Him as King, here is what He said: "Blessed be the King that cometh in the name of the Lord: peace in heaven, and glory in the highest. And some of the Pharisees from among the multitude said unto him, Master, rebuke thy disciples. And He answered and said unto them, I tell you that, if these should hold their peace, the stones would immediately cry out" (Luke 19:38–40).

This marked the end of our Lord's overt three-year earthly ministry. There is a parable in Luke Chapter 13.

He spake also this parable; A certain man had a fig tree planted in his vineyard; and he came and sought fruit thereon, and found none. Then said he unto the dresser of his vineyard, Behold, these three years I come seeking fruit on this fig tree, and find none: cut it down; why cumbereth it the ground? And he answering said unto him, Lord, let it alone this year also, till I shall dig about it, and dung it: And if it bear fruit, well: and if not, then after that thou shalt cut it down. (Luke 13:6–9)

Despite the thousands of souls won to Christ fifty days after the crucifixion at Pentecost and the days following, the majority of Israel, especially among her leaders, rejected Christ. "He came unto his own, and his own received him not" (John 1:11).

Even today, only about 2% of the nation Israel is Christian. The extra year was granted, but a year later, insufficient fruit was produced, and at the stoning of Stephen, the Jews blasphemed the Holy Spirit. At this point God would have been justified in pouring out His wrath in the prophesied day of the Lord. However, God in matchless grace, interrupted prophecy and brought in the Intermission of Grace! We find the prophecy for the day of the Lord from Joel Chapter 2 rerecorded in Acts Chapter 2:

And it shall come to pass afterward, that I will pour out my spirit upon all flesh; and your sons and your daughters shall prophesy, your old men shall dream dreams, your young men shall see visions: And also upon the servants and upon the handmaids in those days will I pour out my spirit. And I will shew wonders in the heavens and in the earth, blood, and fire, and pillars of smoke. The sun shall be turned into darkness, and the moon into blood, before the great and the terrible day of the LORD come. And it shall come to pass, that whosoever shall call on the name of the LORD shall be delivered. (Joel 2:28–32)

And it shall come to pass in the last days, saith God, I will pour out of my Spirit upon all flesh: and your sons and your daughters shall prophesy, and your young men shall see visions, and your old men shall dream dreams: And on my servants and on my handmaidens I will pour out in those days of my Spirit; and they shall prophesy:

(Intermission of Grace)

And I will shew wonders in heaven above, and signs in the earth beneath; blood, and fire, and vapour of smoke: The sun shall be turned into darkness, and the moon into blood, before that great and notable day of the Lord come: And it shall come to pass, that whosoever shall call on the name of the Lord shall be saved. (Acts 2:17–21)

From the context this was to be a continuous process where, if the Jews had accepted their Messiah, the day of the Lord would have eventually begun with the revealing of the Antichrist, and the seven-year tribulation, ending with the battle of Armageddon, and ushering in the thousand-year millennial reign of Christ, followed by the battle of Gog and Magog, the White Throne Judgment, the lake of fire, and the establishment of the eternal state with the new heaven, the new earth, and the new Jerusalem.

The Intermission of Grace consists of the setting aside of the nation Israel (God concluded them all in unbelief.) and taking a new "gospel of the grace of God" directly to Jews and Gentiles alike through a new apostle, Saul of Tarsus, also known as Paul.

For God hath concluded them all in unbelief, that he might have mercy upon all. (Romans 11:32)

For this cause I Paul, the prisoner of Jesus Christ for you Gentiles, If ye have heard of the dispensation of the grace of God which is given me to you-ward: How that by revelation he made known unto me the mystery; (as I wrote afore in few words, Whereby, when ye read, ye may understand my knowledge in the mystery of Christ) Which in other ages was not made known unto the sons of men, as it is now revealed unto his holy apostles and prophets by the Spirit; That the Gentiles should be fellowheirs, and of the same body, and partakers of his promise in Christ by the gospel: Whereof I was made a minister, according to the gift of the grace of God given unto me by the effectual working of his power. Unto me, who am less than the least of all saints, is this grace given, that I should preach among the Gentiles the unsearchable riches of Christ; And to make all men see what is the fellowship of the mystery, which from the beginning of the world hath been hid in God, who created all things by Jesus Christ. (Ephesians 3:1–9; see Appendix III.)

Testifying both to the Jews, and also to the Greeks, repentance toward God, and faith toward our Lord Jesus Christ. And now, behold, I go bound in the spirit unto Jerusalem, not knowing the things that shall befall me there: Save that the Holy Ghost witnesseth in every city, saying that bonds and afflictions abide me. But none of these things move me, neither count I my life dear unto myself, so that I might finish my course with joy, and the ministry, which I have received of the Lord Jesus, to testify the gospel of the grace of God. (Acts 20:21–24)

The simplifying concept referred to earlier is that instead of bringing in the day of the Lord, after the day of Pentecost, as prophesied, God interrupted with the dispensation of the grace of God and its accompanying gospel of the grace of God. This broke down the middle wall of partition and put all mankind on an even plane to be treated with grace. "For he is our peace, who hath made both one, and hath broken down the middle wall of partition between us; Having abolished in his flesh the enmity, even the law of commandments contained in ordinances; for to make in himself of twain one new man, so making peace; And that he might reconcile both unto

God in one body by the cross, having slain the enmity thereby" (Ephesians 2:14–16).

Now, both Jews and Gentiles alike can be saved and reconciled to God by believing the gospel of the grace of God. This new gospel offers the simplest plan of salvation yet and is simply that you believe that Christ died for your sins, was buried, and rose again the third day. "Moreover, brethren, I declare unto you the gospel which I preached unto you, which also ye have received, and wherein ye stand; By which also ye are saved, if ye keep in memory what I preached unto you, unless ye have believed in vain. For I delivered unto you first of all that which I also received, how that Christ died for our sins according to the scriptures; And that he was buried, and that he rose again the third day according to the scriptures" (I Corinthians 15:1–4; see Chapter 2).

It is this believing faith that is all that is required for you to be forgiven all your sins, be saved, and spend eternity with God the Father, God the Son, and God the Holy Spirit. Your works and conduct will be dealt with at the judgment seat of Christ described in Chapter 7.

The sins of both Jews and Gentiles were paid for by Christ's sacrificial death on the cross due to God's grace. Amazing grace!

In the next passage we see that we are saved through faith, and faith in this case is synonymous with believing. The Greek word for faith and belief is *pistis*. "For by grace are ye saved through faith (Greek: *pistis*); and that not of yourselves: it is the gift of God: Not of works, lest any man should boast. For we are his workmanship, created in Christ Jesus unto good works, which God hath before ordained that we should walk in them" (Ephesians 2:8–10).

The same Greek word is used in the next passages translated "believeth" and "believe." "To declare, I say, at this time his righteousness: that he might be just, and the justifier of him which believeth (Greek: *pistis*) in Jesus" (Romans 3:26). "But we are not of them who draw back unto perdition; but of them that believe (Greek: *pistis*) to the saving of the soul" (Hebrews 10:39).

Notice, that in verse 10 of Ephesians 2 that we are "created in Christ Jesus unto good works, which God hath before ordained that we should walk in them." The "Not of works," in verse 8 means that there are no works required in the gospel of the grace of God, but "that we should walk in them."

Many things that were required for salvation, prior to the Intermission of Grace, were taken out of the way after the cross.

Works.

> For what saith the scripture? Abraham believed God, and it was counted unto him for righteousness. Now to him that worketh is the reward not reckoned of grace, but of debt. But to him that worketh not, but believeth on him that justifieth the ungodly, his faith is counted for righteousness. (Romans 4:3–5)

> Who hath saved us, and called us with an holy calling, not according to our works, but according to his own purpose and grace, which was given us in Christ Jesus before the world began. (II Timothy 1:9)

> Not by works of righteousness which we have done, but according to his *mercy* he saved us, by the washing of regeneration, and renewing of the Holy Ghost. (Titus 3:5)

Mercy is not getting what you deserve. *Justice* is getting what you deserve. *Grace* is getting something you do not deserve. Praise God for showing His love for us by His mercy leading to His grace!

Animal Sacrifices. "For it is not possible that the blood of bulls and of goats should take away sins" (Hebrews 10:4).

Water Baptism. "For Christ sent me not to baptize, but to preach the gospel: not with wisdom of words, lest the cross of Christ should be made of none effect" (I Corinthians 1:17).

Today, under grace, we are all baptized (a spiritual baptism or identification with other believers) by the Holy Spirit into a joint body of Christ made up of all believers, in the gospel of the grace of God. The root meaning for the word *baptism* is identification. There are twelve baptisms recorded in Scripture, and only three refer to the water ceremony, to prepare the Jews for the priesthood. (See Appendix I.)

> For by one Spirit are we all baptized into one body, whether we be Jews or Gentiles, whether we be bond or free; and have been all made to drink into one Spirit. (I Corinthians 12:13)
>
> There is one body, and one Spirit, even as ye are called in one hope of your calling; One Lord, one faith, one baptism, One God and Father of all, who is above all, and through all, and in you all. But unto every one of us is given grace according to the measure of the gift of Christ. (Ephesians 4:4–7)

The next three pages have charts that will help diagram and lay out details of the Intermission of Grace.

25

Act One **Old Testament** **Old Covenant**	Creation Original Sin Covenant with Adam Covenant with Noah Covenant with Abraham Establishment of the Nation Israel Covenant with Moses Giving of the Law God's reign through the Judges Man's reign through the Kings Covenant with King David
Act Two - Begins **New Testament** **New Covenant**	Birth of Jesus Christ Earthly Ministry of Jesus Christ Twelve Apostles Gospel of the Kingdom to the Jew first Water Baptism Crucifixion Resurrection Day of Pentecost Stoning of Stephen
Intermission **of Grace**	Heavenly Ministry of Jesus Christ thru Apostle Paul's Ministry Dispensation of Grace (Mystery) Gospel of the Grace of God Spiritual Baptism Joint Body of Jews and Gentiles Rapture of Believers before Wrath
Act Two - Continues **New Testament** **New Covenant**	Anti-Christ Revealed 7 Year Covenant Two Witnesses 144,000 Jewish Evangelists Seven Churches in Asia False Prophet 7 Year Covenant Broken Mark of the Beast Second Coming of Christ Battle of Armageddon 1,000 Year Millennial Kingdom Battle of Gog and Magog White Throne Judgment Lake of Fire
Finale **Eternal State**	New Heaven New Earth New Jerusalem

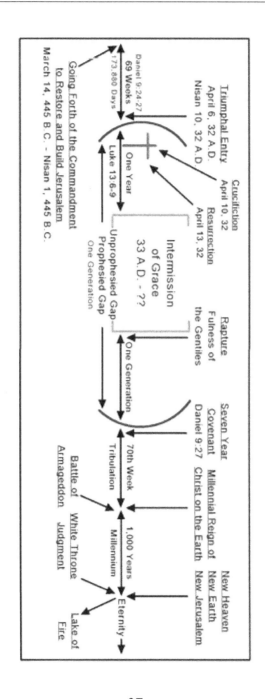

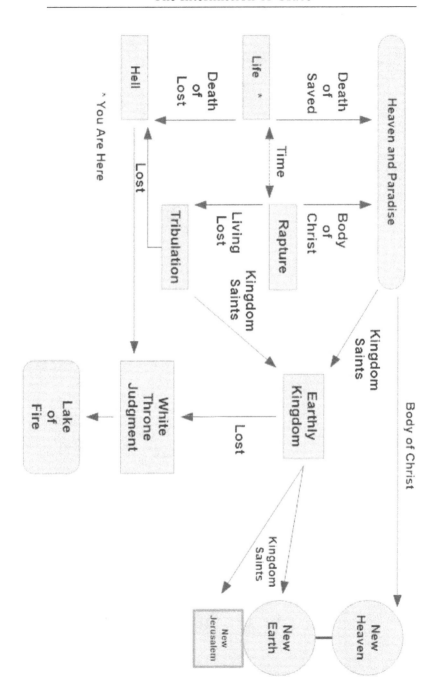

CHAPTER 2

The Plan of Salvation

Potentially, one of the most confusing aspects of Christianity is just exactly how does one become saved and receive the gift of eternal life? The reason for the confusion is there have been various requirements needed to be met, depending on which program of God you look at, over time. We could separate the segments of time into the following categories:

1. Pre-Law
2. Law, Pre-Cross
3. Law, Post-Cross
4. Grace

Let us look at these one at a time:

Pre-Law. Before the giving of the Law through Moses, God required that men and women believe Him and be obedient to Him. To be saved meant that one sought the Lord and believed and obeyed whatever it was that He said. For example, Cain and Abel were asked to bring an offering and apparently Cain was disobedient because ". . . the Lord had respect unto Abel and to his offering:

But unto Cain and to his offering he had not respect. . ." (Genesis 4:4–5). We learn in Hebrews 11:4 "By faith Abel offered unto God a more excellent sacrifice than Cain, by which he obtained witness that he was righteous." Also, we read in I John 3:12, "Not as Cain, who was of that wicked one, and slew his brother. And wherefore slew he him? Because his own works were evil, and his brother's righteous." In every program it has been required that one demonstrate faith by believing in and being obedient to God. Back to Hebrews Chapter 11, we find examples involving not only Cain and Abel, but Enoch, Noah, Abraham, Sara, Isaac, Jacob, Joseph, Rahab, Gideon, Barak, Samson, David, and Samuel. Verse 6 states, "But without faith it is impossible to please Him," and the people mentioned all demonstrated believing faith to obtain righteousness. We will also see, as we move ahead, that the noun *faith* and the verb *believe* both come from the same root word, in the original languages of Hebrew and Greek. "And he (Abraham) believed in the Lord and He counted it to him for righteousness" (Genesis 15:6).

Another requirement from God, before the giving of the Law, was for the males to be circumcised. This was part and parcel of the covenant God made with Abraham, and his seed to inherit the land the Lord would give them, and that He would multiply their seed exceedingly.

Law, Pre-Cross. After the giving of the Law, God set up a priesthood and required blood sacrifices, administered by the priests, to cover sins until the time of the Messiah, who would provide the final and complete blood sacrifice. The Law also contained over 600 commandments, regulations, and ordinances to be followed to demonstrate believing faith and obedience to God.

Law, Post-Cross. Once the Lord Jesus Christ provided the ultimate sacrifice, the animal sacrifices were to cease (at least for the time being) and the requirements for salvation were simplified. According to the pattern that was started to be laid out by Jesus Christ, in His earthly ministry, the people in the nation Israel were to confess their sins, repent, and be water baptized. On the day of Pentecost following the cross, the apostle Peter presented the gospel of the kingdom to his hearers. "Then Peter said unto them, Repent, and be baptized every one of you in the name of Jesus Christ for the remission of sins, and ye shall receive the gift of the Holy Ghost" (Acts 2:38).

Although the initial response was about three thousand souls that were added to the kingdom church that day, the majority of Israel, and especially those among their leaders, rejected this gospel, and began to persecute those who did respond by believing. At the stoning of Stephen, God began to change His dealings with mankind, and began to usher in His heavenly program through His raising up of the apostle Paul.

Grace. The heavenly program that is now in effect further simplified the plan of salvation. The author has from time to time asked members of the clergy to help form a list of all the things that are required for a person to be sure they are going to heaven when they die. The list includes some familiar items, some of which were certainly requirements at one time or another. Top on the list is usually repent and confess your sins. These and the rest are mostly based on Scripture as we have seen. Next are the following in no particular order: water baptism, attending church, tithing, doing good works and being a good person, Holy Communion, making Christ Lord of your life, asking Him into your heart, confessing Him before men, obeying the Ten Commandments, praying regularly, reading the Bible regularly. Now, every one of these things can be good and should be part of our

31

Christian walk, but they have nothing to do with being saved in the first place. In one recent conversation with a pastor, to make a list of requirements for salvation, he asked me, after the list was "complete," what I would have for an answer. I responded that I believe Scripture teaches that you can boil the gospel of the grace of God down to one word: BELIEVE! Romans 4:5 makes it clear: "But to him that worketh not, but believeth on him that justifieth the ungodly, his faith is counted for righteousness."

In Ephesians 2:8–10 we find God's position on salvation. "For by grace are ye saved through faith; and that not of yourselves: it is the gift of God: Not of works, lest any man should boast. For we are his workmanship, created in Christ Jesus unto good works, which God hath before ordained that we should walk in them." You will notice that good works are a result of being saved; being saved is not a result of good works.

Perhaps, the clearest presentation of the gospel of the grace of God, is found in I Corinthians 15:1–4: "Moreover, brethren, I declare unto you the gospel which I preached unto you, which also ye have received, and wherein ye stand; By which also ye are saved, if ye keep in memory what I preached unto you, unless ye have believed in vain. For I delivered unto you first of all that which I also received, how that Christ died for our sins according to the scriptures; And that He was buried, and that He rose again the third day according to the scriptures."

Our natural human, prideful, tendency is that we want to do "our little part" to assist in becoming saved. It is hard for us to understand how God's grace can work independently of our "works" to produce salvation. God's grace is an outgrowth of His love that is completely one-sided and was ultimately made manifest at the cross. "But God commendeth his love toward us, in that, while we were yet sinners, Christ died for us" (Romans 5:8).

The book of Galatians gives us a complete seminar on how grace is intended to work in this dispensation of the grace of God. Paul had gone to the churches in Galatia with the gospel of the grace of God. They rejoiced to find out about God's love for them in that He provided the payment in full for their sins so they could be declared righteous in His sight. But then some Jews from Jerusalem, who were saved under the kingdom gospel, came to those churches and tried (by using Scripture) to have the Galatians come under the Law of Moses and submit to the rite of circumcision.

The upshot of the whole letter to the Galatians is that if anyone tries to add on to the cross of Christ any further requirements than believing that Christ died for your sins, was buried, and rose again the third day, it is a violation of grace and represents "another gospel." The result of this error is that of being accursed which is the opposite of being blessed. As a result of being taken in by this false teaching, the Galatians had lost their blessedness.

Another symptom of adding to grace is confusion. Would you say that today we have lost our blessedness and are confused in our churches? There is much contention about church doctrine, as a result of trying to improperly mix the kingdom program in with the grace program, just like the Jews were doing with the Galatians, two thousand years ago by telling them they needed to be circumcised and come under the Law of Moses (Acts 15:5).

Today, there is not a problem with circumcision, as in Paul's day, but we have plenty of other add-ons, listed earlier, as unnecessary requirements for salvation. Just as those Jews were using Scripture, as sincere believers in Christ, so many among us today are doing the same thing by trying to bring us back under a works-based system of salvation, by adding requirements from a previous program to God's message of pure grace for today. God is not going to have anyone in heaven boasting about all the wonderful things they did to help get themselves there! "And ye are complete in Him" (Colossians 2:10).

The Three Tenses of Salvation

"Moreover, brethren, I declare unto you the gospel which I preached unto you, which also ye have received, and wherein ye stand; By which also ye are saved (present tense—you are saved from the power of sin and false doctrine), if ye keep in memory what I preached unto you, unless ye have believed in vain. For I delivered unto you first of all that which I also received, how that Christ died for our sins according to the scriptures; And that He was buried, and that He rose again the third day according to the scriptures" (I Corinthians 15:1–4).

The three tenses of salvation are:

1. Past—were saved from the penalty of sin
2. Present—are saved from the power of sin and false doctrine
3. Future—will be saved from the presence of sin

The above passage teaches that if you have received (believed by faith) the gospel that Christ died for your sins, was buried, and rose again the third day, you were (past tense), at that time, eternally saved from the penalty of sin, will be (future tense) saved from the presence of sin when you get to heaven, and are (present tense) saved from the power of sin and false doctrine now, as you keep in memory what it is that you believed, so that you won't have believed in vain (when it comes to your Christian walk).

Verse 2 has troubled many a Christian by seeming to suggest that, they must continue to believe a certain way to remain saved from the penalty of sin, or else their faith is in vain. What the verse is really saying can be twofold:

First is that the power of sin now will be lessened to the extent that you keep in memory what Christ did for you, that He paid the penalty for your sins, and that will provide a sin-free environment for you in heaven someday. It is a universal truth that memorized Scripture helps guard against committing sin: "Thy word have I hid in mine heart, that I might not sin against thee" (Psalm 119:11).

Paul was inspired to write that even our faith and doctrine should lead to godliness: "Paul, a servant of God, and an apostle of Jesus Christ, according to the faith of God's elect, and the acknowledging of the truth which is after godliness" (Titus 1:1). "If any man teach otherwise, and consent not to wholesome words, even the words of our Lord Jesus Christ, and to the doctrine which is according to godliness" (I Timothy 6:3).

Second, verse 2 could include being delivered from error or false doctrine if (or as) one keeps in memory, what is stated in verses 3 and 4 concerning the death, burial, and resurrection of Christ.

In checking the Greek for verse 2, the words "are saved" are in the present tense, in all available Greek texts, suggesting that Paul was inspired to write concerning the power of sin in verse 2. In fact, the whole verse is identical in the following Greek texts: *sode'-zo*, σωζεσθε, to save—(Present 5774, Passive 5786, Indicative 5791):

35

δι ου και σωζεσθε τινι λογω ευηγγελισαμην υμιν ει
κατεχετε εκτος ει μη εικη επιστευσατε (ETRG)

δι ου και σωζεσθε τινι λογω ευηγγελισαμην υμιν ει
κατεχετε εκτος ει μη εικη επιστευσατε (GM)

δι ου και σωζεσθε τινι λογω ευηγγελισαμην υμιν ει
κατεχετε εκτος ει μη εικη επιστευσατε (GWH)

Also, you will notice that the word translated "if" in our verse 2 is the Greek word "ει" which, grammatically speaking, is a primary particle of conditionality, a conjunction, that could be translated *"forasmuch as,"* as it is in the book of Acts, Chapter 11, verse 17. *"Forasmuch* (Greek "ει") then *as* God gave them the like gift as He did unto us, who believed on the Lord Jesus Christ; what was I, that I could withstand God?"

If this were done, it would indicate that the writer was acknowledging that they were already keeping in memory what Christ had done for them to be saved (or delivered) from the power of sin (or false doctrine) now, rather than warning them to be sure to keep in memory what He had done for them going forward, if they wanted to be saved from the penalty of sin.

A stronger Greek word for "if" is *ean* (εαν), and as it is used below, it has more the idea of a definite "if" and could have been used (but wasn't) by the Holy Spirit in I Corinthians 15:2. "For circumcision verily profiteth, if (Greek: εαν) thou keep the law: but if (Greek: εαν) thou be a breaker of the law, thy circumcision is made uncircumcision" (Romans 2:25).

It is sad to think about, but some Christians believe the gospel and become sanctified saints, but stop there and soon their memory fades, and they fall back into a similar mode that they were in prior to receiving salvation. In the first letter to the Corinthians, Chapter 1, verse 2, the apostle Paul addresses "the church of God which is at Corinth, to them that are sanctified in Christ Jesus, called to be saints." But look what has happened to them by Chapter 3. "And I, brethren, could not speak unto you as unto spiritual, but as unto carnal, even as unto babes in Christ. I have fed you with milk, and not with meat: for hitherto ye were not able to bear it, neither yet now are ye able. For ye are yet carnal: for whereas there is among you envying, and strife, and divisions, are ye not carnal, and walk as men? For while one saith, I am of Paul; and another, I am of Apollos; are ye not carnal?" (I Corinthians 3:1–4).

In Ephesians, Chapter 4, verse 13, Paul addresses why we need to "all come in the unity of the faith, and of the knowledge of the Son of God, unto a perfect man, unto the measure of the stature of the fulness of Christ."

He goes on to say in verse 14 "That we henceforth be no more children, tossed to and fro, and carried about with every wind of doctrine, by the sleight of men, and cunning craftiness, whereby they lie in wait to deceive."

No matter how you view our passage from I Corinthians 15:1–4, "if" (or) "forasmuch as," you understand the blessings of the three tenses of salvation, and you have the clearest expression of the gospel of the grace of God found in Scripture. Arm yourself with it and you will have an effective tool for sharing the easily understandable method, whereby anyone can be saved from all manner of sin!

CHAPTER 3

Heart vs. Mouth

If thou shalt hearken unto the voice of the LORD thy God, to keep his commandments and his statutes which are written in this book of the law, and if thou turn unto the LORD thy God with all thine heart, and with all thy soul. For this commandment which I command thee this day, it is not hidden from thee, neither is it far off. It is not in heaven, that thou shouldest say, Who shall go up for us to heaven, and bring it unto us, that we may hear it, and do it? Neither is it beyond the sea, that thou shouldest say, Who shall go over the sea for us, and bring it unto us, that we may hear it, and do it? But the word is very nigh unto thee, in thy mouth, and in thy heart, that thou mayest do it. (Deuteronomy 30:10–14)

But what saith it? The word is nigh thee, even in thy mouth, and in thy heart: that is, the word of faith, which we preach; That if thou shalt confess with thy mouth the Lord Jesus, and shalt believe in thine heart that God hath raised him from the dead, thou shalt be saved. For with the heart man believeth unto righteousness; and with the mouth confession is made unto salvation. For the scripture saith, Whosoever believeth on him shall not be ashamed. For there is no difference between the Jew and the Greek: for the same Lord over all is rich unto all that call upon him. For whosoever shall call upon the name of the Lord shall be saved. (Romans 10:8–13)

The whole context of Romans 10:8–13 is where Paul is making a connection between the heart and the mouth. He is drawing from a passage in Deuteronomy 30:10–14, which refers to the Law (verse 10), and applies the connection between the heart and the mouth to the "word of faith" in Romans 10:8. Notice, the similarity of the wording in Deuteronomy 30:14 to that of Romans 10:8.

The whole idea, I believe the Holy Spirit would have us glean from these verses, is that if you believe the gospel that Christ died for your sins, was buried, and rose again the third day, your heart and your mouth will be in agreement. In other words, if you honestly believe with your heart, your mouth (words) will agree (assent) with what your heart believes.

The Greek word translated "confess" in Romans 10:9 above is *homologeo* and it carries the idea of assent and acknowledge. Here are three translations of verse 9 from versions previous to the King James Version of 1611: John Wycliffe Bible, 1384; John Purvey Bible, 1395; and Tyndale Bible, 1534:

> That if thou acknowledge in thy mouth the Lord Jesus Christ, and believest in thine heart, that God raised him from the dead thou shalt be safe (Wycliffe, 1384).

> That if thou acknowledge in thy mouth the Lord Jesus Christ, and believest in thine heart, that God raised him from death, thou shalt be safe (Purvey, 1395).

> This word is the word of faith which we preach. For if thou shalt knowledge with thy mouth that Jesus is the Lord and shalt believe with thine heart that God raised him up from death, thou shalt be safe (Tyndale, 1534).

I had an opportunity a few years ago to witness to a man that I had known for over 10 years. I always remembered him as being the most profane man I had ever met. As I listened to him in his usual mode of profanity, I was praying that I would get an opening to share the gospel with him. Somehow, we got talking about health issues (he is over age 80) and I asked him what he thought would happen to him after he died. He did not immediately give an answer, but it did open the topic of what he had been taught in church services he had attended years earlier. I helped him remember about Christ and the cross and that by believing that He died for his sins that he could be in heaven after death. I then asked him if he believed that Christ died for his sins and he said that he did. I do not know if this was the first time he believed the gospel, but for rest of my visit, I did not hear one more swear word! I now believe that he is saved because it was clear that his heart and mouth were in agreement before I left that day.

I do not think we are to glean the idea that you must believe in your heart, and also confess with your mouth, in order to complete the process of becoming saved. Your mouth, however, will give assent and acknowledge that you are now indwelt by the Holy Spirit. It could very well be that you will verbalize your faith before others, although not necessary for salvation. The instant you believe in your heart that the Lord Jesus Christ died for your sins, was buried, and rose again the third day, you are saved, baptized, and sealed by the Holy Spirit into the body of Christ for eternity and, at least initially, your mouth will begin to show evidence of that believing faith. The reason it is difficult to tell, on the spur of the moment, whether or not someone is saved is that, once saved, a person can fail to appropriate all they have in Christ.

They can fail to get into the Word, so they can start to be led by the Holy Spirit, to begin to display evidence of the fruit of the Spirit. In the story above, the man may have been saved years earlier, but then had drifted back into the works of the flesh (See Galatians 5:16–21) due to a lack of follow-up on his part and by whomever might have shared the gospel with him. You could receive salvation while attending a Billy Graham Crusade, but never read the Bible, associate with other believers, or attend a church service to grow in your faith. If you simply resume your usual mode of life, you could reach the point where you are dominated by the flesh instead of being led by the Spirit (spiritual). Paul refers to these as "carnal" and "babes in Christ" (I Corinthians 3:1).

Verse 17 from the Galatians, Chapter 5, passage mentioned above, describes this condition. "For the flesh lusteth against the Spirit, and the Spirit against the flesh: and these are contrary the one to the other: so that ye cannot do the things that ye would" (Galatians 5:17).

The idea here is that there is a constant warfare going on within all believers. If you are yielding to the flesh you cannot do the things that pertain to being led by the Spirit. Conversely, if you are being led by the Spirit, you cannot do the things that pertain to being led by the flesh.

There is a story about an Eskimo who lived in a remote area of Alaska. He would only make it into the nearest town for supplies about once a month, with the help of a sled and a team of sled dogs. Two of the dogs were opposites in color; one was black, and the other one was white. They were also at odds disposition-wise. Every time they were left alone for a short time, they would get into a fight until one of them would "yield" to the other. The Eskimo was in the habit of making bets with the town's people on which dog would win the conflict. Sometimes, it was the white dog, and other times it was the black dog. This went on for several months with the Eskimo always winning the bet by being able to accurately predict which one of the dogs would win out every time. After a few more visits, with no bets, the town's people convinced the Eskimo to tell them how he was able to predict the outcome so accurately. He simply told them that the one he wanted to win was the one he fed the most. Isn't that just like our struggle with the flesh against the Spirit? We all know very well how to feed the flesh, and we feed the Spirit by studying the Word of God and fleeing sinful activities. Paul writes in Romans 13:14, "But put ye on the Lord Jesus Christ, and make not provision for the flesh, to fulfil the lusts thereof."

This means we do not expose ourselves to those things that would be contrary to the Spirit; we consciously avoid them. On the other hand, we can make provision for the Spirit by feeding on the Word of God, which is breathed by the Spirit. When we learn all the depth of the magnificent gift of God's grace that demonstrates His love and goodness, we respond to overcome temptation and repent from fleshly activities out of gratitude, not out of fear of punishment. Gratitude, based on your love of God, is a much more powerful motivator to good works than fear can ever be. Paul writes in Romans 2:4, "Or despisest thou the riches of his goodness and forbearance and long-suffering; not knowing that the goodness of God leadeth thee to repentance?"

Here is a thought—if you combine loving gratitude with the promise and expectation of receiving rewards, at the judgment seat of Christ, you have a double motivation to live for the Lord, because we know that, "There is therefore now no condemnation to them which are in Christ Jesus, who walk not after the flesh, but after the

Spirit" (Romans 8:1). The phrase "who walk not after the flesh, but after the Spirit" is not found in all Greek manuscripts, and many theologians believe that it was a "gloss" meaning that was added and was not part of the original inspired Word of God. We know that for believers there is no fear of punishment, other than the loss of rewards, for those Christians who do sometimes walk after the flesh, and therefore, the word "condemnation" does not seem to apply. Food for thought.

In this chapter, Paul is writing about the judgment and the goodness of God, and I believe the point is that goodness wins out over the fear of judgment, in motivating us to avoid the deeds of the flesh. Just think of a person who works for a real domineering, stingy, and mean business owner. When the owner is out of town, does that person feel compelled to work extra hard to help build the owner's business? Probably not as much as the person would who works for a gracious, generous, and kind business owner. God is a kind and righteous God. His judgment will be righteous and deserving for those who have not received, by believing, His gift of salvation that demonstrates His grace, love, and goodness. Your salvation is not a result of your good works, but your good works are a result of your salvation. Praise God for His goodness!

CHAPTER 4

The Church(es)

This chapter will show that the word *church* is generic and can apply to the "church in the wilderness" under Moses, the kingdom church under the twelve apostles, or the church, the body of Christ, under the apostle Paul.

The English word *church* is only found in the New Testament of our Bibles. It is translated from the Greek noun, *ekklesia*: a calling out, assembly, church. The Greek word is translated *assembly* three times, *church* seventy-seven times, and *churches* thirty-seven times. There has been much confusion, over the centuries, about when the current church began, and therefore, which church is being referred to at any particular time.

To demonstrate that the use of the Greek word *ekklesia* is generic, it can be shown from the three translations into our English word, *assembly*. This occurs in Acts 19:32, 39, and 41 and refers to an unruly and unlawful assembly. Further proof can be shown in Acts 7:38, where our word *church* refers to the "church in the wilderness" under Moses. "This is he, that was in the church in the wilderness with the angel which spake to him in the mount Sina, and with our fathers: who received the lively oracles to give unto us" (Acts 7:38).

The Kingdom Church

The kingdom church was a continuation of the church of the Old Testament, before Christ, and the church in the New Testament, after Christ. This is evidenced by the reference in Acts 2:47 on the day of Pentecost where we read, "Then they that gladly received his word were baptized: and the same day there were added unto them about three thousand souls" (Acts 2:41).

It is a common misconception that the current church began on the day of Pentecost, but those converts were added to the existing church at that time. Moreover, the first offer of the long-awaited kingdom was to come in the apostle Peter's second Pentecostal address in Acts 3. "Repent ye therefore, and be converted, that your sins may be blotted out, when the times of refreshing shall come from the presence of the Lord; And he shall send Jesus Christ, which before was preached unto you: Whom the heaven must receive until the times of restitution of all things, which God hath spoken by the mouth of all his holy prophets since the world began" (Acts 3:19–21).

After all, in Matthew 3:2 John the Baptist began to preach: "Repent ye: for the kingdom of heaven is at hand." Christ also sent the Twelve forth in Matthew 10:7 to preach: "The kingdom of heaven is at hand." We can see from the parable in Luke 19:12, that this kingdom was to be given to Christ, in heaven by God, and brought back to earth to be set up. The promise for the Jews to become priests in the kingdom from heaven, however, was a conditional one as we learn from Exodus 19. "Now therefore, if ye will obey my voice indeed, and keep my covenant, then ye shall be a peculiar treasure unto me above all people: for all the earth is mine: And ye shall be unto me a kingdom of priests, and an holy nation. These are the words which thou shalt speak unto the children of Israel" (Exodus 19:5–6).

To this day, Christ has not returned to set up that kingdom, because the majority of Israel, especially among her leaders, rejected the gospel of the kingdom. This brings us to the next church in the Bible, which is the one we are under today.

The Church, the Body of Christ

As we approach the mid-part of the book of Acts, we find the earthly, prophetic, kingdom program of God being interrupted by His heavenly, mystery, body-of-Christ program, through the apostle Paul. Beginning in the mid-part of the book of Acts and extending from the book of Romans through the book of Philemon, most of the uses of the word *church* are for the church which is His body. This marks the true beginning of the current church, which was between the 9th and 13th Chapters of the book of Acts. After the rapture of the present church, the book of Hebrews is a transition back to the kingdom program and kingdom church, where you ultimately see all Israel being saved, and Christ returning in the second coming with the promised kingdom. "And hath put all things under his feet, and gave him to be the head over all things to the church, Which is his body, the fulness of him that filleth all in all" (Ephesians 1:22–23).

Note, during Paul's ministry of approximately 30 years, both the gospel of the kingdom and the gospel of the grace of God were running concurrently. To avoid confusion during this present age, until the Lord returns, it is best to properly identify the church being referred to, by adding either kingdom, or body of Christ, with its reference.

The Commissions that Go with the Churches
and Gospels

Just as there are two churches and two gospels, there are two commissions that go with each church and gospel.

The kingdom church and kingdom gospel have a commission usually known as the Great Commission:

> And Jesus came and spake unto them, saying, All power is given unto me in heaven and in earth. Go ye therefore, and teach all nations, baptizing them in the name of the Father, and of the Son, and of the Holy Ghost: Teaching them to observe all things whatsoever I have commanded you: and, lo, I am with you always, even unto the end of the world. Amen. (Matthew 28:18–20) (Note: Many theologians believe that this is mainly a future commission.)

> And he said unto them, Go ye into all the world, and preach the gospel to every creature. He that believeth and is baptized shall be saved; but he that believeth not shall be damned. And these signs shall follow them that believe; In my name shall they cast out devils; they shall speak with new tongues; They shall take up serpents; and if they drink any deadly thing, it shall not hurt them; they shall lay hands on the sick, and they shall recover. (Mark 16:18–20)

> And said unto them, Thus it is written, and thus it behoved Christ to suffer, and to rise from the dead the third day: And that repentance and remission of sins should be preached in his name among all nations, beginning at Jerusalem. And ye are witnesses of these things. And, behold, I send the promise of my Father upon you: but tarry ye in the city of Jerusalem, until ye be endued with power from on high. (Luke 24:46–49)

When we come to the church, the body of Christ, and the gospel of the grace of God, we find a two-part commission, usually known as the Grace Commission:

Part one:

> Unto me, who am less than the least of all saints, is this grace given, that I should preach among the Gentiles the unsearchable riches of Christ; And to make *all men* see what is the *fellowship* of the mystery, which from the beginning of the world hath been hid in God, who created all things by Jesus Christ. (Ephesians 3:8–9)

There are two Greek words supplied for the word fellowship, above, depending on which Greek manuscript you use. The King James Version, mostly based on the Textus Receptus, uses the Greek word: *koininia*, translated *fellowship*. In the original the word means participation, communion. Other English versions, based on the Majority Text and the Wescott Hort Text, use the word dispensation or administration translated from the Greek word, *oikonomia*, which in the original means dispensation, stewardship. Whether we endeavor to make all men see the fellowship, dispensation, or administration of the mystery, it will be the same Grace Commission to which we are referring.

Ephesians 3:9

> KJV: And to make all men see what is the *fellowship* of the mystery, which from the beginning of the world hath been hid in God, who created all things *by Jesus Christ*.

> EGTR: και φωτισαι παντας τις η **κοινωνια** του μυστηριου του αποκεκρυμμενου απο των αιωνων εν τω θεω τω τα παντα κτισαντι δια ιησου χριστου

GM: και φωτισαι παντας τις η **οικονομια** του μυστηριου του αποκεκρυμμενου απο των αιωνων εν τω θεω τω τα παντα κτισαντι δια ιησου χριστου

GWH: και φωτισαι παντας τις η **οικονομια** του μυστηριου του αποκεκρυμμενου απο των αιωνων εν τω θεω τω τα παντα κτισαντι (Notice that this Greek text omits *"by Jesus Christ."*)

Part two:

And all things are of God, who hath reconciled us to himself by Jesus Christ, and hath given to us the ministry of reconciliation; To wit, that God was in Christ, reconciling the *world* unto himself, not imputing their trespasses unto them; and hath committed unto us the word of reconciliation. Now then we are ambassadors for Christ, as though God did beseech you by us: we pray you in Christ's stead, be ye reconciled to God. For he hath made him to be sin for us, who knew no sin; that we might be made the righteousness of God in him. (II Corinthians 5:18–21)

As ambassadors for Christ, we can be assured that God will call us, His ambassadors, home in the rapture, before He declares war on the earth in the coming seven-year tribulation. We see a parallel in our governments today, that before a country declares war on another country, their ambassadors are called home. This Grace Commission is a glorious message, from God, that we are to take to all men and the world.

CHAPTER 5

The Gospel(s)

This Chapter will show that the word *gospel* is generic and can apply to the gospel of the kingdom, the gospel of the grace of God, or the everlasting gospel.

The English word *gospel* is only found in the New Testament of our Bibles. It is translated from the Greek noun, *euaggelion*: gospel, and the verb, *euaggelizo*: declare glad. Essentially, it is the good news of mankind being able to obtain salvation from God. There has been much confusion, over the centuries, about the concept of salvation, and therefore, much confusion about the word *gospel*.

Let us begin by looking at the various provisions, over time, God has made in order to offer salvation to mankind. In the Garden of Eden at the first temptation, provided by the serpent, Adam and Eve sinned, and God promised to send the "Seed" that would bruise the serpent's head (Genesis 3:15). We now know that this was Christ, when He made the full payment for all the sins of all believing mankind, with His death on the cross. In the meantime, God shed blood to cover the sin of Adam and Eve, when he made coats of skins and clothed them, until the fulfillment of the promise of the "Seed" (Genesis

3:21). There were offerings brought to God also, at this time (Genesis 4:3–5). Later, after the flood, and after the Tower of Babel, altars were built, and men called on the name of the Lord (Genesis 12:8).

Next, through Abraham, God began a people with whom He could have dealings. These became known as the nation Israel. God gave them the Law through Moses, which consisted of more than 600 commandments, regulations, and ordinances. God also instituted a priesthood with a blood sacrificial system and water cleansing ceremony of atoning (covering) for the sins of the nation Israel (Exodus 29:1–4; 10–11). This system spanned 1,500 years, until the time of the Messiah.

The Gospel of the Kingdom

At the advent of Jesus Christ, the gospel of the kingdom was preached to the nation Israel. It consisted of confession of sins, repentance, and the water cleansing ceremony known as baptism. The declaration in this gospel was that the kingdom of (from) heaven was at hand. The nation Israel had been given a conditional promise by God, at the giving of the Law, that they all could become a kingdom of priests (Exodus 19:5–6). For 1,500 years only specific members of the tribe of Levi could serve in the priesthood. Now, if the nation Israel confessed their sins, repented of their broken covenant relationship, and submitted to the water cleansing ceremony, baptism, they all could become that kingdom of priests.

After the death, burial, and resurrection of the Lord Jesus Christ, the gospel of the kingdom continued with a change to acknowledge that the final blood sacrifice had been offered by Him for all who would believe. Now, the nation Israel was to confess, repent, and be baptized, in the name of Jesus Christ, for the remission of sins, and they would receive the gift of the Holy Spirit (Acts 2:38). It is apparent that the apostle Peter and his hearers did not fully understand the significance of the blood sacrifice of our Lord, since Peter preached the bad news of the cross (Acts 2:23, 36). Things were looking good, at this point, as 3,000 plus 5,000 men responded to the gospel of the kingdom. In Peter's next sermon/address he lessened the charge of murder, by acknowledging their ignorance, and literally offered the kingdom to the nation Israel (Acts 3:17–21). This kingdom would consist of Jesus Christ returning to earth to establish the long-awaited time about which the Old Testament writers had written from the time of Moses through Malachi.

It was at this point that we start to see a change in the proceedings. The leaders in Israel began to fear the rise of this new teaching of the gospel of the kingdom and started persecuting the apostles who were preaching this gospel. Despite this persecution God allowed the program to go unchanged, for one year, until the stoning of Stephen. It was at that time that the nation Israel resisted or blasphemed the Holy Spirit. This was their third and last chance to be reconciled to God. One, they had rejected God by demanding a king under Samuel; two, they rejected Christ at the cross; and three, they rejected the Holy Spirit at the stoning of Stephen (Acts 7:51–60).

The Gospel of the Grace of God

At this point God changed the program of His dealings with mankind and ushered in the gospel of the grace of God through the apostle Paul. The terms of salvation, in this gospel, are believing in the death, burial, and resurrection of the Lord Jesus Christ and that He died for our sins. God also temporarily set aside His dealings with the nation Israel, exclusively, and offered this gospel to the Jew and Gentile alike. (Ephesians 2:16)

The difference in this gospel is that Christ's blood, and His blood alone, is sufficient payment for all past, present, and future sins of those who believe this gospel of God's grace. The entire body of truth for this new program was revealed to the apostle Paul, in a series of direct heavenly revelations, from the Lord Jesus Christ, over a period of about 30 years. Paul calls it the mystery and progressively explains it to us in his thirteen epistles, Romans through Philemon. The books of Acts and Hebrews are transitional to go from the gospel of the kingdom to the gospel of the grace of God and back again. (See chart on page 14.)

The Everlasting Gospel

The everlasting gospel will be preached, by angels, just prior to the battle of Armageddon and will most likely consist of the good news that Christ has overcome sin, with His blood sacrifice on the cross, and is about to overcome His enemies, in the upcoming battle (Revelation 14:6–7).

In the meantime, we still have the privilege of declaring the good news of the gospel of the grace of God to anyone who will listen, because God has thrown open wide the gates of heaven to all, during this program of His grace. You will want to arm yourselves with Scripture like the following: Romans 10:9–13, I Corinthians 15:1–4, Ephesians 2:8-10.

Are there Two Different Gospels in Scripture?

To translate the Greek genitive (possessive) case for nouns into English, there are two primary choices. You can either add *of* before the noun or add *'s* to the end of the noun.

In Galatians 2:7 both nouns, uncircumcision (ακροβυστιας) and circumcision (περιτομης), are in the genitive (possessive) case in all available Greek texts, validating the use of "of" in the King James Version & the English Revised Version. This correctly indicates that the two gospels are not the same gospel. We first have the "gospel of the grace of God" (uncircumcision), followed by the "gospel of the kingdom" (circumcision). All one needs to do is read the two gospels in Scripture, to understand the difference.

Gospel of the Kingdom (Circumcision)—King James Version: "Then Peter said unto them, Repent, and be baptized every one of you in the name of Jesus Christ for the remission of sins, and ye shall receive the gift of the Holy Ghost" (Acts 2:38).

And the precursor to the gospel of the kingdom (all nations to be blessed in the future kingdom): "Ye are the children of the prophets, and of the covenant which God made with our fathers, saying unto Abraham, And in thy seed shall all the kindreds of the earth be blessed" (Acts 3:25). "And the scripture, foreseeing that God would justify the heathen through faith, preached before the gospel unto Abraham, saying, In thee shall all nations be blessed" (Galatians 3:8).

Gospel of the Grace of God (uncircumcision)—King James Version.

> Moreover, brethren, I declare unto you the gospel which I preached unto you, which also ye have received, and wherein ye stand; By which also ye are saved, if ye keep in memory what I preached unto you, unless ye have believed in vain. For I delivered unto you first of all that which I also received, how that Christ died for our sins

according to the scriptures; And that he was buried, and that he rose again the third day according to the scriptures. (I Corinthians 15:1–4)

For by grace are ye saved through faith; and that not of yourselves: it is the gift of God: Not of works, lest any man should boast. (Ephesians 2:8–9)

But contrariwise, when they saw that the gospel *of* the uncircumcision was committed unto me, as the gospel *of* the circumcision was unto Peter. (Galatians 2:7 KJV, true to the Greek genitive case))

ERV (true to the Greek genitive case): "But contrariwise, when they saw that I had been entrusted with the gospel *of* the uncircumcision, even as Peter with the gospel *of* the circumcision."

NKJV (not true to the Greek genitive case): "But on the contrary, when they saw that the gospel for the uncircumcised had been committed to me, as the gospel for the circumcised was to Peter."

EGTR: αλλα <235> {CONJ} τουναντιον <5121> {ADV-K} ιδοντες <3708> (5631) {V-2AAP-NPM} οτι <3754> {CONJ} πεπιστευμαι <4100> (5769) {V-RPI-1S} το<3588> {T-ASN} ευαγγελιον <2098> {N-ASN} της < 3588> {T-GSF} ακροβυστιας <203> {N-GSF}* καθως <2531> {ADV} πετρος <4074> {N-NSM} της <3588> {T-GSF} περιτομης <4061> {Noun-GSF}*

MTB: αλλα <235> {CONJ} τουναντιον <5121> {ADV-K} ιδοντες <3708> (5631) {V-2AAP-NPM} οτι <3754> {CONJ} πεπιστευμαι <4100> (5769) {V-RPI-1S} το<3588> {T-ASN} ευαγγελιον <2098> {N-ASN} της < 3588> {T-GSF} ακροβυστιας <203> {N-GSF}* καθως

---

* {Noun—Genitive Singular Feminine}

<2531> {ADV} πετρος <4074> {N-NSM} της <3588> {T-GSF} περιτομης<4061> {N-GSF}*

GWH—Alexandrian: αλλα <235> {CONJ} τουναντιον <5121> {ADV-K} ιδοντες <3708> (5631) {V-2AAP-NPM} οτι <3754> {CONJ} πεπιστευμαι <4100> (5769) {V-RPI-1S} το<3588> {T-ASN} ευαγγελιον <2098> {N-ASN} της < 3588> {T-GSF} ακροβυστιας <203> {N-GSF}* καθως <2531> {ADV} πετρος <4074> {N-NSM} της <3588> {T-GSF} περιτομης <4061> {N-GSF}*

I will close with a quote from long-time Grace Pastor, Joel Finck D.D.

It is unfortunate that many modern translations of Scripture have seemingly gone to a great extent to nullify the plain teaching of this verse. Rather than "the gospel of the uncircumcision" and "the gospel of the circumcision," (which clearly shows two separate messages), some translations substitute words such as "the gospel to the Jews" and "the gospel to the Gentiles." This suggests only one message going in two different directions. The problem with these modern translations is that the text actually uses the "genitive" case which is possessive. That is, Paul is speaking of the gospel which belongs to circumcision, and that which belongs to uncircumcision. It is the same construction used over and over in the gospels with the phrase, "gospel of the kingdom." This does not refer to the gospel being preached to the kingdom; instead, it is a gospel that belongs to or pertains to the kingdom. Likewise, the wording here is not a reference to whom it is being preached, but rather the content of the message. Simply put, Paul's gospel did not require the ordinance of circumcision whereas Peter's gospel did.

---

* {Noun—Genitive Singular Feminine}

CHAPTER 6

The Kingdom(s)

This chapter will endeavor to show that the word *kingdom* in the Bible is generic, and can apply to kingdom of God, kingdom of heaven, or heavenly kingdom.

The English word *kingdom* is found throughout the entire Bible. In the New Testament it is translated from the Greek noun *basileia* and is rendered either *kingdom* (150 times), *kingdoms* (4 times), or *reigneth* (1 time). The root definition is royalty and refers to God as King, and most of the references to kingdom(s) pertain to God's kingdom(s). To dispense with the one verse containing our word translated *reigneth*, we will notice it has nothing to do with kingdom or the reigning of God as King. "And the woman which thou sawest is that great city, which reigneth over the kings of the earth" (Revelation 17:18).

The rest of the references (kingdom or kingdoms) fall either into God's earthly program of prophecy or His heavenly program of the mystery. The phrase, kingdom of God, can be used to identify either program, or can also be used to refer to the overall kingdom of God, including both programs. Without the principle of right division, it is futile to try to understand the term *kingdom* in Scripture.

Confusion on this topic can be understood when we further consider that in the book of Matthew, the future earthly kingdom is referred to as *kingdom of heaven* thirty-one times. It is the only place this phrase is used and is a reference to that future earthly kingdom that Christ will receive from the Father in heaven, and will bring with Him from heaven to earth at the second coming. (See the parable in Luke 19:12ff.)

Matthew also uses kingdom of God, as do Mark, Luke, and John in their gospels, for a reference to the future earthly kingdom from God in heaven. Luke also uses *kingdom of God* seven times and *kingdom* one time in the book of Acts, to refer to the earthly kingdom, as well as the combined kingdom of God.

The apostle Paul uses the word *kingdom* in his epistles fourteen times and only one of those refer to the future earthly kingdom (I Corinthians 15:24). The other thirteen times we have reference to the heavenly kingdom as: kingdom of God (8 times), His kingdom (2 times), kingdom of Christ and of God (1 time), kingdom of His dear Son (1 time), and heavenly kingdom (1 time).

Kingdom of God
(Overall Combined Kingdom)

Earthly Kingdom	Heavenly Kingdom
Part of the prophecy program	Part of the mystery program
To occur on earth	To occur in the heavenlies
Called: kingdom of God	Called: kingdom of God
kingdom of heaven	His kingdom
kingdom	kingdom of Christ and of God
	kingdom of His dear Son
	heavenly kingdom

CHAPTER 7

The Judgment Seat of Christ

Just as there will be two future comings of Christ, there will be two future judgments. The next coming of Christ will be at the rapture, after the fullness of the Gentiles has come in, and the last coming will be at the end of the tribulation, at the battle of Armageddon. The next judgment will be at the judgment seat of Christ, and the last judgment will be at the great white throne, after the thousand-year earthly reign of Christ, in the millennial kingdom.

The judgment seat of Christ will most likely be associated with the rapture of the body of Christ, for in I Thessalonians 4:17 we read, "Then we which are alive and remain shall be caught up together with them in the clouds, to meet the Lord in the air: and so shall we ever be with the Lord."

The word *meet* in the original Greek has the meaning of a planned meeting and would therefore accommodate the judgment seat of Christ.

The two direct references to this judgment are found in the Scriptures below.

> But why dost thou judge thy brother? or why dost thou set at nought thy brother? for we shall all stand before the judgment seat of Christ. For it is written, As I live, saith the Lord, every knee shall bow to me, and every tongue shall confess to God. So then every one of us shall give account of himself to God. (Romans 14:10–12)

> For we must all appear before the judgment seat of Christ; that every one may receive the things done in his body, according to that he hath done, whether it be good or bad. (II Corinthians 5:10)

By the nature and timing of this judgment, only believers will be present. Let us look at other relevant Scriptures to get details of the proceedings.

> I have planted, Apollos watered; but God gave the increase. So then neither is he that planteth any thing, neither he that watereth; but God that giveth the increase. Now he that planteth and he that watereth are one: and every man shall receive his own reward according to his own labour. For we are labourers together with God: ye are God's husbandry, ye are God's building. According to the grace of God which is given unto me, as a wise master-builder, I have laid the foundation, and another buildeth thereon. But let every man take heed how he buildeth thereupon. For other foundation can no man lay than that is laid, which is Jesus Christ. Now if any man build upon this foundation gold, silver, precious stones, wood, hay, stubble; Every man's work shall be made manifest: for the day shall declare it, because it shall be revealed by fire; and the fire shall try every man's work of what sort it is. If any man's work abide which he hath built thereupon, he shall receive a reward. If any man's work shall be burned, he shall suffer loss: but he himself shall be saved; yet so as by fire. (I Corinthians 3:6–15)

Fire in this case will probably be the Word of God. (See Jeremiah 20:9 and Luke 24:32.)

> Let a man so account of us, as of the ministers of Christ, and stewards of the mysteries of God. Moreover it is required in stewards, that a man be found faithful. But with me it is a very small thing that I should be judged of you, or of man's judgment: yea, I judge not mine own self. For I know nothing by myself; yet am I not hereby justified: but he that judgeth me is the Lord. Therefore judge nothing before the time, until the Lord come, who both will bring to light the hidden things of darkness, and will make manifest the counsels of the hearts: and then shall every man have praise of God. (I Corinthians 4:1–5)

The rewards (or loss thereof) will be the main consideration at this judgment. We will all give an account of ourselves and receive the things done in our body whether good or bad. It is worthy of note, that even if some of our works are burned, we will be saved, so as by fire. I believe that what this is telling us is that at this judgment, we will dispense with some of the things (works) we have done since becoming saved. All our works will be tested by fire and with six building materials utilized (i.e., gold, silver, precious stones, or wood, hay, stubble) we will all have some works that will burn and some that will abide (Greek, *meno*: remain). My feeling is that it will be a great relief to get rid of the burned works once and for all. The works that remain will constitute a reward and the Bible also speaks about a crown that we will be given. "Henceforth there is laid up for me a crown of righteousness, which the Lord, the righteous judge, shall give me at that day: and not to me only, but unto all them also that love his appearing" (2 Timothy 4:8).

The whole topic of the judgment seat of Christ is important to all believers and especially grace believers, who sometimes are accused of using grace as a license to continue in sin. This is an unfair accusation because grace believers are very familiar with the apostle Paul's teachings in Romans 7 and 8 on this issue. Rather, we are told that we are dead to sin and that the Holy Spirit will help us to overcome sin. What the teaching of the judgment seat of Christ can mean to us is that we have an incentive to live for the Lord, and to flee from the deeds of the flesh in this life. Our eternal reward in heaven, with all its glory, can be built upon while we are still on this earth. Did you ever wonder why God did not just take us to heaven the moment we were saved? He has left us here for a reason—a purpose—and will reward us for our faithful service.

Before we leave this topic, let us address the question of grace versus works. I believe the proper relationship between the two is summarized in Ephesians: "For by grace are ye saved through faith; and that not of yourselves: it is the gift of God: Not of works, lest any man should boast. For we are his workmanship, created in Christ Jesus unto good works, which God hath before ordained that we should walk in them" (Ephesians 2:8–10).

Good works are a result of being saved; being saved is not a result of good works. If we are thankful for God's grace, we will want to do those things that please Him, and in turn He will reward us for our good works.

CHAPTER 8

Forgiveness

When it comes to contradictions in Scripture, there seems to be many unanswerable conflicts. However, most of these seeming impossibilities tend to fade away when you apply the Biblical solution of "right division," based on II Timothy 2:15: "Study to shew thyself approved unto God, a workman that needeth not to be ashamed, rightly dividing the word of truth."

One area of doctrine that can demonstrate this idea of conflicts, is forgiveness. Consider a passage from Matthew. "For if ye forgive men their trespasses, your heavenly Father will also forgive you: But if ye forgive not men their trespasses, neither will your Father forgive your trespasses" (Matthew 6:14–15).

Under the kingdom program, before the cross, one requirement for forgiveness was that you must forgive others, to be forgiven yourself. But, as we will see after the cross, forgiveness is always expressed in the past tense. The forgiveness provided by the cross was instantaneous at the death of Christ, but was not made known until the dispensational change that occurred after Israel rejected the offer of the kingdom, in Acts 3:19–21, and the resultant stoning of Stephen in Acts 7. It was at that time, when the world was ripe for the undiluted wrath of God, that He reached down, in matchless grace, and saved the chief persecutor of Jesus Christ, Saul of Tarsus (also known as Paul). He made Paul an apostle, then offered salvation to Jews and Gentiles alike, through their believing that Christ had died for their sins, was buried, and rose again the third day. As we know from Scripture and history, the majority of Jews and Gentiles rejected (and continue to reject) this new gospel of the grace of God, during this present dispensation of the grace of God (Intermission of Grace).

Luke quoted Paul in Acts 20:24. "But none of these things move me, neither count I my life dear unto myself, so that I might finish my course with joy, and the ministry, which I have received of the Lord Jesus, to testify the *gospel of the grace of God*."

> If ye have heard of the *dispensation of the grace of God* which is given me to you-ward: How that by revelation he made known unto me the mystery; (as I wrote afore in few words, Whereby, when ye read, ye may understand my knowledge in the mystery of Christ) Which in other ages was not made known unto the sons of men, as it is now revealed unto his holy apostles and prophets by the Spirit; That the Gentiles should be fellowheirs, and of the same body, and partakers of his promise in Christ by the gospel. (Ephesians 3:2–6) (See Appendix III.)

In fact, it is still true today, that the majority of believers and non-believers reject that the gospel and dispensation changed about one year after the death of Christ. This explains why we can observe over 400 denominational differences in our churches. Let us look to Scripture for the treatment of forgiveness after the change. "And be ye kind one to another, tenderhearted, forgiving one another, even as God for Christ's sake *hath forgiven* you" (Ephesians 4:32). "Forbearing one another, and forgiving one another, if any man have a quarrel against any: even as Christ *forgave* you, so also do ye" (Colossians 3:13).

You will notice that forgiveness is always in the past tense, during the current program, and this is verified by all available Greek texts. Now, we are admonished to forgive others because we have been forgiven all. What is it for us to forgive comparatively small things of others, when we were forgiven all trespasses through simply believing the gospel of the grace of God? "And you, being dead in your sins and the uncircumcision of your flesh, hath he made alive together with him, *having forgiven* you all trespasses" (Colossians 2:14).

In the following passages, the requirement that you must first forgive before you are forgiven was taken away by the cross:

> Be it known unto you therefore, men and brethren, that through this man is preached unto you the *forgiveness* of sins. (Acts 13:38)

> To open their eyes, and to turn them from darkness to light, and from the power of Satan unto God, that they may receive *forgiveness* of sins, and inheritance among them which are sanctified by faith that is in me. (Acts 26:18)

> In whom we have redemption through his blood, the *forgiveness* of sins, according to the riches of his grace. (Ephesians 1:7)

> In whom we have redemption through his blood, even the *forgiveness* of sins. (Colossians 1:14)

Lest anyone should get the idea that under grace our ability to sin is unlimited, and there are no consequences, let us consider the judgment seat of Christ. Many of our works including unforgiveness are sin. Once you believe the gospel that Christ died for your sins, was buried, and rose again the third day, you are baptized (this should not be confused with the water ceremony under the kingdom program) by the Holy Spirit, with a spiritual baptism (identification) into the body of Christ (among the other believers), and there you are sealed by the Holy Spirit until the day of redemption (Ephesians 4:30). This means that your salvation is secure in Christ, but your rewards can be affected by your conduct. The following verses will outline this process:

> Moreover, brethren, I declare to you the gospel which I preached to you, which also ye have received, and in which ye stand; by which also ye are saved, if ye keep in memory what I preached to you, unless ye have believed in vain. For I delivered to you first of all, that which I also received, that Christ died for our sins, according to the scriptures; and that he was buried, and that he rose again the third day according to the scriptures. (I Corinthians 15:1–4)

> For by grace are ye saved through faith; and that not of yourselves: it is the gift of God: Not of works, lest any man should boast. (Ephesians 2:8–9)

> In whom ye also trusted, after that ye heard the word of truth, the gospel of your salvation: in whom also after that ye believed, ye were sealed with that Holy Spirit of promise. (Ephesians 1:13)

> For by one Spirit are we all baptized into one body, whether we be Jews or Gentiles, whether we be bond or free; and have been all made to drink into one Spirit. (I Corinthians 12:13)

> There is one body, and one Spirit, even as ye are called

in one hope of your calling; One Lord, one faith, one baptism, One God and Father of all, who is above all, and through all, and in you all. (Ephesians 4:4–6)

For we must all appear before the judgment seat of Christ; that every one may receive the things done in his body, according to that he hath done, whether it be good or bad. (II Corinthians 5:10)

I have planted, Apollos watered; but God gave the increase. So then neither is he that planteth any thing, neither he that watereth; but God that giveth the increase. Now he that planteth and he that watereth are one: and every man shall receive his own reward according to his own labour. For we are labourers together with God: ye are God's husbandry, ye are God's building. According to the grace of God which is given unto me, as a wise master-builder, I have laid the foundation, and another buildeth thereon. But let every man take heed how he buildeth thereupon. For other foundation can no man lay than that is laid, which is Jesus Christ. Now if any man build upon this foundation gold, silver, precious stones, wood, hay, stubble; Every man's work shall be made manifest: for the day shall declare it, because it shall be revealed by fire; and the fire shall try every man's work of what sort it is. If any man's work abide which he hath built thereupon, he shall receive a reward. If any man's work shall be burned, he shall suffer loss: but he himself shall be saved; yet so as by fire. (I Corinthians 3:6–15) (Works burned, but still saved. Fire in this case will probably be the Word of God. See Jeremiah 20:9 and Luke 24:32.)

So, under grace we do not lose our salvation if we do not forgive. We will, however, lose rewards, which means that we have an incentive to forgive and avoid all other sins as well. Simply put, our conduct as Christians will have eternal consequences, concerning rewards and loss of rewards. This one recovered truth alone has the potential to remove many barriers to an understanding of how a correct application of Scripture could and would eliminate much of the confusion and bitterness among people of faith that could, would, and should spread to the entire world!

CHAPTER 9

The Rapture, Concept, History, and Evidence

Greek is the original language of our New Testament and you will find the Greek noun *apostasia* used twice. The first occurrence is in Acts 21:21 *apostasian* (accusative case) and the second in II Thessalonians 2:3 *apostasia* (nominative case). When Jerome produced the Latin Vulgate Bible in the year 390, at the direction of Roman Emperor Constantine I, he translated the Greek noun *apostasia* in Acts 21:21, into the Latin noun (in the accusative case)—**discessionem** (withdrawal) and in II Thessalonians 2:3, into the Latin noun (in the nominative case)—**discessio** (withdrawal). The Greek word, *apostasia*, is the noun form of the Greek verb, *aphistemi* (depart).

The two thoughts that can legitimately be derived from the word *apostasia* are:

1. non-physical, such as a departure from a truth or the teaching of a person (Acts 21:21), and
2. physical departure from a location (II Thessalonians 2:3).

I believe that both these thoughts are conveyed in the two occurrences of the Greek word *apostasia* in the Bible. The first occurrence is Acts 21:21, written by Luke. The first two English Bible translations (Wycliffe & Purvey), taken from the Latin Vulgate, render the word "departing." This is using the infinitive or verbal noun form of the Latin noun discessionem. An alternate rendering for Wycliffe & Purvey could have been "withdrawal" to keep it as a noun. So, there we have the non-physical thought of a withdrawal or departing from the teachings of Moses.

Acts 21:21

Jerome's Latin Vulgate Bible—390: "audierunt autem de te quia **discessionem** doceas a Mose eorum qui per gentes sunt Iudaeorum dicens non debere circumcidere eos filios suos neque secundum consuetudinem ingredi" [**discessionem** (noun)—withdrawal].

John Wycliffe Bible—1384: "And they heard of thee, that thou teachest **departing** from Moses of those Jews that be by heathen men, saying, that they owe not to circumcise their sons, neither owe to enter after custom."

John Purvey Bible—1395: "And they heard of thee, that thou teachest **departing** from Moses, of those Jews that be by heathen men, that say, that they owe not to circumcise their sons, neither owe to enter by custom."

Later, three English Bibles were translated from the Erasmus' Greek Textus Receptus and in Acts 21:21 render the Greek word *apostasia*, "forsake." Here again the translators used the infinitive or verbal noun form of the Greek noun *apostasia*. Again, this word is derived from the Greek verb *aphistemi* (depart) but another word that is close is the Greek noun, *stasis* (dissention).

The English word *dissention* is similar looking to the Latin word *discessionem*, and since the Tyndale, Geneva, and KJV translators looked at the Latin as well as the Greek, this could explain where the idea of "forsake" may have originated. You must remember that the truth of the rapture of the church, the body of Christ, was first committed only to the apostle Paul and was mostly lost, as a truth, before the end of the first century. This truth wasn't fully recovered until late in the 1800s so, during the 1500s and 1600s, it's perfectly understandable that there would not have been much thought of a physical departure, when you come to the second occurrence of the word *apostasia*, as the apostle Paul uses it in II Thessalonians 2:3. Even today many Christians aren't aware of the recovered truth of the rapture! So, with the light that has been given since Tyndale, Geneva, and the King James Version, this author believes they should have used the more accurate rendering of "departing" or "withdrawal" or "departure" instead of "forsake."

Acts 21:21

EGTR: "kathchyhsan de peri sou oti *apostasian* didaskeiv apo mwsewv touv kata ta eynh pantav ioudaiouv legwn mh peritemnein autouv ta tekna mhde toiv eyesin peripatein" [*apostasian—Apostasia,* noun, falling away, forsake, (departure)].

William Tyndale Bible—1534: "And they are informed of thee that thou teachest all the Jews which are among the gentiles to **forsake** Moses, and sayest that they ought not to circumcise their children, neither to live after the customs."

Geneva Bible—1560: "Now they are informed of thee, that thou teachest all the Jews, which are among the

Gentiles, to **forsake** Moses, and sayest that they ought not to circumcise their children, neither to live after the customs."

KJV: "And they are informed of thee, that thou teachest all the Jews which are among the Gentiles to **forsake** Moses, saying that they ought not to circumcise their children, neither to walk after the customs."

When we come to II Thessalonians 2:3, this time Jerome translated the Greek noun *apostasia* into the Latin noun (in the nominative or vocative case)—**discessio** (withdrawal). His chosen word renders what I think is the correct thought, of the physical departure or rapture of the believers, to whom Paul was referring. To put the verse into proper context, we need to refer to Paul's first letter in I Thessalonians 1:10 where we read about "Jesus, which delivered us from the wrath to come." The word "delivered" is the Greek word *rhuomai* and is in the Greek present tense, so it has the idea of "delivers." In other words, when the wrath comes, He delivers us. In I Thessalonians 4:16–18 we find the method that He will use when He delivers us. "For the Lord Himself shall descend from heaven with a shout, with the voice of the archangel, and with the trump of God: and the dead in Christ shall rise first: Then we which are alive and remain shall be *caught up* together with them in the clouds, to meet the Lord in the air: and so shall we ever be with the Lord. Wherefore comfort one another with these words."

(**Ladies and gentlemen—this** *caught up* **is the rapture!**)

In II Thessalonians Chapter 2 we find the apostle Paul reminding his readers of "the coming of our Lord Jesus Christ, and by our gathering together unto Him" (in verse 1), and he proceeds (in verse 2) to dispel the false rumor that the wrath, associated with the day of the Lord, had already come. He assures them (in verse 3) that that day will not come before "the *apostasia*." The only logical event he could have been referring to was the "caught up" (from I Thessalonians 4:17), and the "gathering together unto Him" (from II Thessalonians 2:1). It does not make sense that he would tell them that the day of Christ (or the Lord) will not come until there is a falling away or apostasy from the truth. They were already witnessing apostasy via the false reports he was trying to dispel. In the first two English translations, out of the Latin, we find **departing away** and **dissension**. You will notice that Wycliffe italicized the word *dissension*, suggesting that he felt he was adding it to the original Latin. Purvey was a little more direct and only did what is known as a transliteration. This is where a word is not translated but is given a spelling update to conform it to the new language.

II Thessalonians 2:3

Jerome's Latin Vulgate Bible—390: "ne quis vos seducat ullo modo quoniam nisi venerit **discessio** primum et revelatus fuerit homo peccati filius perditionis" [**discessio** (noun)—withdrawal].

John Wycliffe Bible—1384: "That no man deceive you in any manner. For no but **departing away**, or *dissension*, shall come first, and the man of sin be showed, the son of perdition."

John Purvey Bible—1395: "No man deceive you in any manner. For but **dissension** come first, and the man of sin be showed, the son of perdition."

When we read the next English translations of the Greek *apostasia*, we find **a departing** which represents the thought of a physical departure and **a falling away** which represents a non-physical departure from truth. In

75

all available Greek texts (Byzantine: Textus Receptus & Majority; Alexandrian: Wescott Hort) the definite article (the) "h" is present so that a direct translation should be "the" departure (rapture).

II Thessalonians 2:3

EGTR: "mh tiv umav exapathsh kata mhdena tropon oti ean mh elyh h *apostasia* prwton kai apokalufyh o anyrwpov thv amartiav o uiov thv apwleiav."

William Tyndale Bible—1534: "Let no man deceive you by any means, for the Lord cometh not, except there come **a departing** first, and that that sinful man be opened, the son of perdition."

Geneva Bible—1560: "Let no man deceive you by any means, for that day shall not come, except there come **a departing** first, and that the man of sin be disclosed, even the son of perdition."

KJV: "Let no man deceive you by any means: for that day shall not come, except there come **a falling away** first, and that man of sin be revealed, the son of perdition;"

The English Revised Version Bible of 1885, at least, correctly brought the definite article (the) "h" into the translation. "let no man beguile you in any wise: for it will not be, except *the* **falling away** come first, and the man of sin be revealed, the son of perdition."

I knew a woman (she died in 2007), who grew up in Greece, and although the Modern Greek is much changed from the Greek in our New Testaments, many of the words are still in usage today. I asked her about the Greek word *apostasia*, and she told me how her father used it with her. He told her that, if she found herself with others that were talking about things, or doing things of which he did not approve, she was to *apostasia*. At that point she tore a piece from a page of paper in front of her and tossed it across the table. She was to depart from that group! Her father was expressing, by the infinitive or verbal noun use of both the non-physical and physical departing from their ideas, activities, and location.

I do not believe apostasy is the idea either. There are Greek words that would better depict apostasy, e.g., *hairesis*—heresy, disunion. Note, the word apostasy is not used in the KJV, but only in the later English translations of the 1900s.

Finally, I want to address where the word "rapture" came from that so many believers use to identify the "caught up" of I Thessalonians 4:17, and the "departing" of II Thessalonians 2:3. When Jerome produced the Latin Vulgate, he used the Latin verb rapiemur (to seize, snatch, carry away), and when you study all the various tenses (raptus, rapio, rapui, ratum), you can see where a word like "rapture," coined in Middle English in the 1590's, could be used today for *apostasia*.

I Thessalonians 4:17

Jerome's Latin Vulgate Bible—390: "deinde nos qui vivimus qui relinquimur simul **rapiemur** cum illis in nubibus obviam Domino in aera et sic semper cum Domino erimus."

The original Greek manuscripts use the Greek verb *arpaghsomeya* (*harpazo*—catch up, take by force, catch away, pluck) and all available Greek texts agree.

I Thessalonians 4:17

EGTR: "epeita hmeiv oi zwntev oi perileipomenoi ama sun autoiv *arpaghsomeya* en nefelaiv eiv apanthsin tou kuriou eiv aera kai outwv pantote sun kuriw esomeya."

GM: "epeita hmeiv oi zwntev oi perileipomenoi ama sun autoiv *arpaghsomeya* en nefelaiv eiv apanthsin tou kuriou eiv aera kai outwv pantote sun kuriw esomeya."

GWH: "epeita hmeiv oi zwntev oi perileipomenoi ama sun autoiv *arpaghsomeya* en nefelaiv eiv apanthsin tou kuriou eiv aera kai outwv pantote sun kuriw esomeya."

The earliest English Bible translations, i.e., Wycliffe and Purvey, use "snatch (up)" in their translations, and Tyndale, Geneva, and the King James Version use "caught up."

I Thessalonians 4:17

KJV: "Then we which are alive and remain shall be caught up (raptured) together with them in the clouds, to meet the Lord in the air: and so shall we ever be with the Lord."

Geneva Bible—1560: "Then shall we which live and remain, be caught up with them also in the clouds, to meet the Lord in the air, and so shall we ever be with the Lord."

In II Thessalonians 2:3 we find the only time, in Paul's letters, that he uses the Greek word *apostasia*. I believe he had in mind the same physical departure he taught in I Thessalonians chapter 4. It would not make sense that he would talk about a non-physical departure from the truth, or apostasy. There have been major breakouts of apostasy, in virtually every generation of time, since the first century. It would not be very helpful to look for apostasy as a sign that the day of Christ (or the Lord) was about to start. Because Paul was inspired to write in the first letter that believers will be delivered from the wrath to come via the departure (rapture), I believe he was reassuring them, in the second letter, that the rapture will precede the day of the Lord's wrath and that the reports (II Thessalonians 2:2) that "the day of Christ" (or the Lord) was then happening were false. In II Thessalonians 2:5 Paul further reminds them, "Remember ye not, that, when I was yet with you, I told you these things?"

II Thessalonians 2:3

Jerome's Latin Vulgate Bible—390: "ne quis vos seducat ullo modo quoniam nisi venerit **discessio** primum et revelatus fuerit homo peccati filius perditionis" [**discessio** (noun)—withdrawal, dispersal].

KJV: "Let no man deceive you by any means: for that day shall not come, except there come **a falling away** the* rapture first, and that man of sin be revealed, the son of perdition."

Geneva Bible—1560: "Let no man deceive you by any means, for that day shall not come, except there come **a departing** first, and that the man of sin be disclosed, even the son of perdition."

EGTR: "mh tiv umav exapathsh kata mhdena tropon oti ean mh elyh h* *apostasia* prwton kai apokalufyh o anyrwpov thv amartiav o uiov thv apwleiav" [*apostasia*, noun, falling away, forsake (departure)].

GM: "mh tiv umav exapathsh kata mhdena tropon oti ean mh elyh h* *apostasia* prwton kai apokalufyh o anyrwpov thv amartiav o uiov thv apwleiav."

GWH: "mh tiv umav exapathsh kata mhdena tropon

---

* Note, all 3 Greek texts have the definite article (the) "h" preceding the word *apostasia*.

oti ean mh elyh h* *apostasia* prwton kai apokalufyh o anyrwpov thv anomiav o uiov thv apwleiav."

The timing of the rapture is up to God and the main hint we have as to its occurrence is in Romans 11:25–26 where we read, "For I would not, brethren, that ye should be ignorant of this mystery, lest ye should be wise in your own conceits; that blindness in part is happened to Israel, *until* the *fulness* of the Gentiles be come in. And so all Israel shall be saved: as it is written, There shall come out of Sion the Deliverer, and shall turn away ungodliness from Jacob."

The Greek word for "fulness" is *pleroma*, meaning, "which is put in to fill up"—completion. The "blindness" won't come off Israel *until* the day of the Lord, when "all Israel shall be saved," which will be after the rapture. This means that God is longsuffering while he waits for the completed number, which only He knows, of Gentiles (and Jews) being saved that He can enjoy an eternal relationship with as sons and daughters, that are conformed to the image of His Son. (See Chapter 16.)

It is understandable that most of our English translations have missed the idea of a physical departure or rapture from II Thessalonians 2:3, because the truth of the pretribulational rapture was mostly lost during the first century. Since that time, we have been guided by "the tradition of men" and "the rudiments of the world." I think it is high time we return to the truth in our churches and comfort each other with the Biblically supportable truth of the rapture. "And that, knowing the time, that now it is high time to awake out of sleep: for now is our salvation nearer than when we believed" (Romans 13:11).

* Note, all 3 Greek texts have the definite article (the) "h" preceding the word *apostasia*.

CHAPTER 10

The Faith of Christ

Even the righteousness of God which is by faith of Jesus (*ihsou Iesous*: genitive) Christ (*cristou Christos*: genitive) unto all and upon all them that believe: for there is no difference. (Romans 3:22)

Knowing that a man is not justified by the works of the law, but by the faith of Jesus (*Iesous*: genitive) Christ (*Christos*: genitive), even we have believed in Jesus Christ, that we might be justified by the faith of Christ (*Christos*: genitive), and not by the works of the law: for by the works of the law shall no flesh be justified. (Galatians 2:16)

I am crucified with Christ: nevertheless I live; yet not I, but Christ liveth in me: and the life which I now live in the flesh I live by the faith of the Son (*uiou huios*: genitive) of God, who loved me, and gave himself for me. (Galatians 2:20)

But the scripture hath concluded all under sin, that the promise by faith of Jesus (genitive) Christ (genitive) might be given to them that believe. (Galatians 3:22)

In whom we have boldness and access with confidence by the faith of him (*autou autos*: genitive). (Ephesians 3:12)

And be found in him, not having mine own righteousness, which is of the law, but that which is through the faith of Christ (genitive), the righteousness which is of God by faith. (Philippians 3:9)

Buried with him in baptism, wherein also ye are risen with him through the faith of the operation (energeiav energeia: genitive) of God, who hath raised him from the dead. (Colossians 2:12)

To translate the Greek genitive case for nouns into English, there are two primary choices. You can either add *of* before the noun or add *'s* to the end of the noun. In order for any of the above to be translated "faith in," there would have to be present the Greek word for "in," which is "*en*," and there are none. The King James Version has it right on all of these, and virtually all modern translations have substituted the word "in" for "of," and the difference may be subtle, but is also especially important.

Faith has two aspects: objective, and subjective. Our faith is objective, and His faith is subjective; He is the object of our faith. It would be foolish for us to have faith in One Who did not keep faith or to be faithful to One Who was not faithful. Christ demonstrated His faith when "He humbled Himself, and became obedient unto death, even the death of the cross" (Philippians 2:8b). Our faith, as important as it is to salvation, is secondary to the faith of Christ. His faith, demonstrated by the cross, is what paid the price for our sins, by the offering of Himself. Our faith (believing) is what appropriates that payment for our sins personally. We can put our faith in Him only because He is so faithful.

CHAPTER 11

Eternal Security

As we approach the topic of eternal security (whether or not you can lose your salvation once saved), we look back in history to find that, after the Protestant Reformation in the sixteenth century, this topic was among those that caused wars to be fought and men to be burned at the stake. It is certain that Satan did not want truth to be rediscovered further than was already brought out by this Reformation (justification by faith alone, in Christ alone).

Pauline Truths Lost (Order of Loss)

First: The Distinctive Message & Ministry of the Apostle Paul—II Timothy 1:15

Second: The Pre-Tribulational Rapture of the Church, the body of Christ

Third: The Difference between Israel and the Church, the body of Christ

Fourth: Justification by Faith Alone, in Christ Alone— Acts 13:39

Pauline Truths Recovered (Order of Recovery)

First: Justification by Faith Alone, in Christ Alone
        Recovered via Protestant Reformation in the
        16th Century via Luther, et al.
Second: The Difference between Israel and the Church,
        the body of Christ
        Recovered in the 1800s via John Nelson
        Darby, Ethelbert William Bullinger, Sir Robert
        Anderson, et al.
Third: The Pre-Tribulational Rapture of the Church,
        the body of Christ
        Recovered in the 19th Century via John Nelson
        Darby and included by C.I. Scofield in his
        Reference Bible, published 1909.
Fourth: The Distinctive Message & Ministry of the
        Apostle Paul
        Recovered from the middle 1900s via John
        C. O'Hair, Charles F. Baker, Cornelius R.
        Stam, et al.

As you can see from the chart above, the four truths, from the ministry of Paul, were lost for fifteen hundred years, and recovered over a period of about three hundred fifty years. During this whole process, the multitude of confusion was due to not recognizing the distinctive message and ministry of the apostle Paul (the last of the truths recovered). Without the principle of right division of the Scriptures, one is left in an incorrect denominational view, based on which parts of the former prophetic program are improperly mixed with the current mystery program.

God ushered in a new program of pure grace with the apostle Paul, and many things changed. For example, where Israel had an earthly kingdom hope, we now have a heavenly calling and hope: "For our conversation

84

(Greek, *politeuma*: community, citizenship) is in heaven; from whence also we look for the Saviour, the Lord Jesus Christ: Who shall change our vile body, that it may be fashioned like unto his glorious body, according to the working whereby he is able even to subdue all things unto himself" (Philippians 3:20–21).

The terms of salvation in the former program, were to repent, confess sins, and be water baptized for the remission of their sins. The current program requires only that we believe in the death, burial, and resurrection of the Lord Jesus Christ and that He died for our sins: "Moreover, brethren, I declare unto you the gospel which I preached unto you, which also ye have received, and wherein ye stand; By which also ye are saved, if ye keep in memory what I preached unto you, unless ye have believed in vain. For I delivered unto you first of all that which I also received, how that Christ died for our sins according to the scriptures; And that he was buried, and that he rose again the third day according to the scriptures" (I Corinthians 15:1–4).

There is nothing you can add to the finished work of Christ on the cross, that will earn your salvation. By the same token, there is nothing you can or need to do, after being saved, to keep yourself saved. It is by grace and is a gift of God.

Some teach that once you are saved, you can lose your salvation if you do certain things (or do not do certain things). This is a result of a failure to recognize that Ephesians 2:8–9 says, "For by grace are ye saved through faith; and that not of yourselves: it is a gift of God: not of works, lest any man should boast." This passage goes on to say in the next verse, Ephesians 2:10, "For we are his workmanship, created in Christ Jesus unto good works, which God hath before ordained that we should walk in them." Good works are a result of being saved; being saved is not a result of good works. Simply put, you committed no sin so big that the cross of Christ could not pay the price to save you; and after being saved, there is no sin so big that the cross of Christ cannot pay that price as well.

By improperly mixing the two programs of God, many denominations tend to teach that we must do something to help earn our salvation, and likewise, we must do something to help keep it. The enemy cannot cause you to lose your salvation but, if he can keep you uncertain of having it, then he can keep you from understanding the truth and seeking the spiritual growth you could otherwise gain. Also, this uncertainty can keep you from sharing the gospel with others, as the Spirit leads you.

Before we leave this important topic, let us search the Scriptures to see if one can be secure in Christ. There is one verse, one of the more familiar in the Bible, which says it all: "For God so loved the world, that he gave his only begotten Son, that whosoever believeth in him should not perish, but have everlasting life" (John 3:16). In what sense is everlasting life everlasting if you can lose it?

The next two verses add to the thought "For God sent not his Son into the world to condemn the world; but that the world through him might be saved. He that believeth on him is not condemned: but he that believeth not is condemned already, because he hath not believed in the name of the only begotten Son of God" (John 3:17–18).

In Hebrews 10:14 we read, "For by one offering he hath perfected for ever them that are sanctified."

Let us look to the Pauline record to see this truth for us: "Therefore being justified by faith, we have peace with God through our Lord Jesus Christ" (Romans 5:1). "In whom ye also trusted, after that ye heard the word of truth, the gospel of your salvation: in whom also after that ye believed, ye were sealed with that holy Spirit of promise, Which is the earnest of our inheritance until the redemption of the purchased possession, unto the praise of his glory" (Ephesians 1:13–14).

Once you have believed, you are sealed with the Holy Spirit, and that seal is stronger than the power of sin in your life.

Some object to the teaching of being eternally secure by observing that many so-called Christians seem to be as evil and as sin-ridden as non-believers. First of all, it is not for us to know for sure who is saved among us. Look at the example of Judas. He was one of the Twelve and was an impostor, about whom Christ said in John 6:70, "Have not I chosen you twelve, and one of you is a devil?" Secondly, even we, as blood-bought, justified, and sealed believers, will continue to sin, due to our flesh, our sin nature. Let us verify this with a lamentation by the apostle Paul himself:

> For we know that the law is spiritual: but I am carnal, sold under sin. For that which I do I allow not: for what I would, that do I not; but what I hate, that do I. If then I do that which I would not, I consent unto the law that it is good. Now then it is no more I that do it, but sin that dwelleth in me. For I know that in me (that is, in my flesh,) dwelleth no good thing: for to will is present with me; but how to perform that which is good I find not. For the good that I would I do not: but the evil which I would not, that I do. Now if I do that I would not, it is no more I that do it, but sin that dwelleth in me. I find then a law, that, when I would do good, evil is present with me. For I delight in the law of God after the inward man: But I see another law in my members, warring against the law of my mind, and bringing me into captivity to the law of sin which is in my members.

> O wretched man that I am! who shall deliver me from the body of this death? I thank God through Jesus Christ our Lord. So then with the mind I myself serve the law of God; but with the flesh the law of sin. (Romans 7:14–25)

We will not be rid of sin until we are caught up to be with the Lord, and evil is defeated once and for all. "For the wages of sin is death; but the gift of God is eternal life through Jesus Christ our Lord" (Romans 6:23). Again, in what sense is eternal life eternal if you can lose it? "Not by works of righteousness which we have done, but according to his *mercy* he saved us, by the washing of regeneration, and renewing of the Holy Ghost" (Titus 3:5).

Justice: getting what we deserve; *mercy*: not getting what we deserve; *grace*: getting what we do not deserve; praise God for His mercy and grace toward us by His love, through Christ!

> I am crucified with Christ: nevertheless I live; yet not I, but Christ liveth in me: and the life which I now live in the flesh I live by the faith of the Son of God, who loved me, and gave himself for me. (Galatians 2:20)

> And ye are complete in him, which is the head of all principality and power: In whom also ye are circumcised with the circumcision made without hands, in putting off the body of the sins of the flesh by the circumcision of Christ: Buried with him in baptism, wherein also ye are risen with him through the faith of the operation of God, who hath raised him from the dead. And you, being dead in your sins and the uncircumcision of your flesh, hath he quickened together with him, having forgiven you *all* trespasses; Blotting out the handwriting of ordinances that was against us, which was contrary to us, and took it out of the way, nailing it to his cross; And having spoiled principalities and powers, he made a shew of them openly, triumphing over them in it. (Colossians 2:10–15)

I took the liberty of italicizing the word *all* above and take it to mean all past, present, and future sins.

"For I am persuaded, that neither death, nor life, nor angels, nor principalities, nor powers, nor things present, nor things to come, Nor height, nor depth, nor any other creature, shall be able to separate us from the love of God, which is in Christ Jesus our Lord" (Romans 8:38–39).

God wants us to know for sure that nothing can separate us from His love! The enemy would have you to believe that one or more certain types of sins will cause you to become separated from God's love.

Some denominations teach that we must confess our sins, after being saved, in order to have them forgiven. This is based on a verse from I John: "If we confess our sins, he is faithful and just to forgive us our sins, and to cleanse us from all unrighteousness" (I John 1:9).

Read that chapter carefully. First, this verse is addressing non-believers; and second, John was writing to Israel under the kingdom gospel, where they were to repent (confess their sins), and be water baptized for their remission. Moreover, during the tribulation, this same gospel of the kingdom will be preached in all the world, and then the end will come. To this date, this gospel of the kingdom has not been preached in all the world, since it was replaced with the gospel of the grace of God. "And this gospel of the kingdom shall be preached in all the world for a witness unto all nations; and then shall the end come" (Matthew 24:14). "John did baptize in the wilderness, and preach the baptism of repentance for the remission of sins. And there went out unto him all the land of Judaea, and they of Jerusalem, and were all baptized of him in the river of Jordan, confessing their sins" (Mark 1:4–5).

CHAPTER 12

The Baptisms

Water baptism, as we see being used in many churches today, has its origin during the exodus of the Jews from Egypt, around the giving of the Law. We read in Exodus 19:5–6 that if Israel kept the covenant, that they would become a kingdom of priests. This is the first hint of the future kingdom that was spoken of later by the prophets. At the time of these verses, only specific members of the tribe of Levi could be eligible for the priesthood. Now, however, all Israel was given a conditional promise that they could all become priests in the future kingdom. Exodus 19:5–6: "Now therefore, if ye will obey my voice indeed, and keep my covenant, then ye shall be a peculiar treasure unto me above all people: for all the earth is mine: And ye shall be unto me a kingdom of priests, and an holy nation. These are the words which thou shalt speak unto the children of Israel."

This promise was later confirmed to Israel in the following verses:

> But ye are a chosen generation, a royal priesthood, an holy nation, a peculiar people; that ye should shew forth the praises of him who hath called you out of darkness into his marvellous light. (I Peter 2:9)

Thou art worthy to take the book, and to open the seals thereof: for thou wast slain, and hast redeemed us to God by thy blood out of every kindred, and tongue, and people, and nation; And hast made us unto our God kings and priests (kingdom of priests): and we shall reign on the earth. (Revelation 5:9–10)

Blessed and holy is he that hath part in the first resurrection: on such the second death hath no power, but they shall be priests of God and of Christ, and shall reign with him a thousand years. (Revelation 20:6)

There was a blood and water ceremony required for the priests, from the tribe of Levi, to observe before being placed into the priesthood.

And this is the thing that thou shalt do unto them to hallow them, to minister unto me in the priest's office: Take one young bullock, and two rams without blemish, And unleavened bread, and cakes unleavened tempered with oil, and wafers unleavened anointed with oil: of wheaten flour shalt thou make them. And thou shalt put them into one basket, and bring them in the basket, with the bullock and the two rams. And Aaron and his sons thou shalt bring unto the door of the tabernacle of the congregation, and shalt wash them with water. (Exodus 29:1–4)

And thou shalt cause a bullock to be brought before the tabernacle of the congregation: and Aaron and his sons shall put their hands upon the head of the bullock. And thou shalt kill the bullock before the LORD, by the door of the tabernacle of the congregation. (Exodus 29:10–11)

Later, in a prophecy by Ezekiel, Israel was told of a future day

For I will take you from among the heathen, and gather you out of all countries, and will bring you into your own land. Then will I sprinkle clean water upon you, and ye shall be clean: from all your filthiness, and from all your idols, will I cleanse you. A new heart also will I give you, and a new spirit will I put within you: and I will take away the stony heart out of your flesh, and I will give you an heart of flesh. And I will put my spirit within you, and cause you to walk in my statutes, and ye shall keep my judgments, and do them. And ye shall dwell in the land that I gave to your fathers; and ye shall be my people, and I will be your God. (Ezekiel 36:24–28)

It would appear that sprinkling was the method used in the water ceremony, later to be known as baptism. Fast forward now to the time of John the Baptist and the preaching of the kingdom at hand. Israel was now ready to become that kingdom of priests if they would confess their sins, repent, and submit to water baptism.

In those days came John the Baptist, preaching in the wilderness of Judaea, And saying, Repent ye: for the kingdom of heaven is at hand. For this is he that was spoken of by the prophet Esaias, saying, The voice of one crying in the wilderness, Prepare ye the way of the Lord, make his paths straight. And the same John had his raiment of camel's hair, and a leathern girdle about his loins; and his meat was locusts and wild honey. Then went out to him Jerusalem, and all Judaea, and all the region round about Jordan, And were baptized of him in Jordan, confessing their sins. (Matthew 3:1–6)

From that time Jesus began to preach, and to say, Repent: for the kingdom of heaven is at hand. (Matthew 4:17)

The majority in the nation Israel did not repent and submit to water baptism. (Luke 7:29-30) After the stoning of Stephen (the last strike), the kingdom program was temporarily set aside and the current program, called the mystery, was ushered in through the apostle Paul. Water baptism has no part in the mystery; however, we are identified with or baptized, by the Spirit, into a new joint body called the body of Christ. "For by one Spirit are we all baptized into one body, whether we be Jews or Gentiles, whether we be bond or free; and have been all made to drink into one Spirit" (I Corinthians 12:13).

This is in accordance with the unity (i.e., the oneness) we have in Christ during the present program of God's grace. Here again, if we rightly divide the Scriptures, we see that whereas the kingdom program was replaced by the mystery; consequently, water baptism was replaced by a Spirit(ual) baptism, or identification, with a new body, the body of Christ. "There is one body, and one Spirit, even as ye are called in one hope of your calling; One Lord, one faith, one baptism, One God and Father of all, who is above all, and through all, and in you all" (Ephesians 4:4–6).

During the early ministry of the apostle Paul, water baptism was practiced as were the gifts of the Spirit. This was the program he came out of and it took about 30 years for him to receive all the revelations, from Jesus Christ, pertaining to the new program, the mystery. In his first letter to the Corinthians, we find Paul writing about the fact that water baptism and the gifts of the spirit were to be replaced with something better. Concerning the gifts of the Spirit, we learn that once all the revelations he was receiving were completed, the gifts would "cease," "vanish," or be "done away." (See I Corinthians 13:8–10.) Concerning water baptism, he starts out in the first chapter by explaining that although he and the others had been water baptizing, he was not sent to baptize, but to preach the gospel. So, with the gospel of the grace of God replacing the gospel of the kingdom, water baptism was being replaced by the one Spirit(ual) baptism administered by the Spirit the moment we believe the gospel (See the two passages just above.) "For Christ sent me not to baptize, but to preach the gospel: not with wisdom of words, lest the cross of Christ should be made of none effect" (I Corinthians 1:17).

Oh, my dear brothers and sisters in Christ, how understanding this one truth, concerning baptism, from Scripture would remove much confusion in our churches today! For in our current assemblies there is foisted upon us "tradition of men" and "rudiments of the world" as to who gets water baptized, when, at what age, and by what method; whether by sprinkling, dipping, pouring, or immersion. (Compare the verse above with the one below.) Today, there is no one majority view on the method of water baptism: "Beware lest any man spoil you through philosophy and vain deceit after the *tradition of men*, after the *rudiments of the world,* and not after Christ" (Colossians 2:8).

Let us close this chapter by hearing what our Lord had to say about such things in Mark 7:7–9, 13: "Howbeit in vain do they worship me, teaching for doctrines the commandments of men. For laying aside the commandment of God, ye hold the *tradition of men*, as the washing of pots and cups: and many other such like things ye do. And he said unto them, Full well ye reject the commandment of God, that ye may keep your own tradition. . . Making the word of God of *none effect* through your tradition, which ye have delivered: and many such like things do ye."

CHAPTER 13

Three Days and
Three Nights

H ave you ever wondered how we can observe Good
Friday, as the day our Savior was crucified, and also
celebrate His resurrection on the following Sunday? After
all, He Himself predicted that He would be in the heart
of the earth for three days and three nights: "For as Jonas
was three days and three nights in the whale's belly; so
shall the Son of man be three days and three nights in the
heart of the earth" (Matthew 12:40).

No matter how hard you try, you can only fit two
days and two nights into the Good Friday time frame,
since He arose before dawn on Sunday.

This chapter will endeavor to clear up the confusion
and, in doing so, we are going to discover an amazing
fulfillment of prophecy that will pinpoint the actual
Passion Week, so we will be able to literally see where the
three days and three nights fit into our Lord's final week.

Our first stop is a prophecy given through Daniel in
Chapter 9 verse 25 in the year 538 BC. "Know therefore and understand, that from the going forth of the
commandment to restore and to build Jerusalem *unto the*

Messiah the Prince shall be seven weeks, and threescore and two weeks: the street shall be built again, and the wall, even in troublous times" (Daniel 9:25).

Ninety-three years later we read in Nehemiah Chapter 2:1–6:

> And it came to pass in the month Nisan, in the twentieth year of Artaxerxes the king, that wine was before him: and I took up the wine, and gave it unto the king. Now I had not been beforetime sad in his presence. Wherefore the king said unto me, Why is thy countenance sad, seeing thou art not sick? this is nothing else but sorrow of heart. Then I was very sore afraid, And said unto the king, Let the king live for ever: why should not my countenance be sad, when the city, the place of my fathers' sepulchres, lieth waste, and the gates thereof are consumed with fire? Then the king said unto me, For what dost thou make request? So I prayed to the God of heaven. And I said unto the king, If it please the king, and if thy servant have found favour in thy sight, that thou wouldest send me unto Judah, unto the city of my fathers' sepulchres, that I may build it. And the king said unto me, (the queen also sitting by him,) For how long shall thy journey be? and when wilt thou return? So it pleased the king to send me; and I set him a time. (Nehemiah 2:1–6)

King Artaxerxes reigned in Persia from 465 BC to 424 BC and the first day of the month Nisan in his 20th year is equivalent to our March 14, 445 BC.

Now, let us crunch the numbers. Daniel identified a total of 69 weeks of years (Genesis 29:27), which amounts to 69 times in 7 years, times 360 days, in the Jewish year. Thus 69 x 7 x 360 = 173,880 days counting from March 14, 445 BC *unto the Messiah the Prince*. During our Lord's early years, on the earth, He warned His disciples and others not to make Him known (Matthew 12:16;

Mark 3:12). But there was one day it was declared, "Blessed be the King that cometh in the name of the Lord: peace in heaven, and glory in the highest." Immediately, "some of the Pharisees from among the multitude said unto Him, Master, rebuke thy disciples." But this time, "He answered and said unto them, I tell you that, if these should hold their peace, the stones would immediately cry out" (Luke 19:38–40). This day was none other than the day ("unto the Messiah the Prince") we call the "triumphal entry" and "Palm Sunday," when He rode into Jerusalem on a colt. We will be able to see that it was on April 6, 32 AD, which is exactly 173,880 days from March 14, 445 BC!

Tiberius Caesar Augustus lived from November 16, 42 BC to March 16, 37 AD and he reigned from August 19, 14 AD to March 16, 37 AD. Thus, when we read of a reference to the *fifteenth year of the reign*, we can identify the time frame of: August 19, 28 AD to April 19, 29 AD (to the Passover). From the following passage from Luke, we know that during this time, our Lord began His three-year earthly ministry, after being baptized by John the son of Zacharias. We also know that he was crucified on the Passover, three years later, as we will see in a moment.

> Now in the *fifteenth year of the reign* of Tiberius Caesar, Pontius Pilate being governor of Judaea, and Herod being tetrarch of Galilee, and his brother Philip tetrarch of Ituraea and of the region of Trachonitis, and Lysanias the tetrarch of Abilene, Annas and Caiaphas being the high priests, the word of God came unto John the son of Zacharias in the wilderness. And he came into all the country about Jordan, preaching the baptism of repentance for the remission of sins; As it is written in the book of the words of Esaias the prophet, saying, The voice of one crying in the wilderness, Prepare ye the way of the

Lord, make his paths straight. And as the people were in expectation, and all men mused in their hearts of John, whether he were the Christ, or not; John answered, saying unto them all, I indeed baptize you with water; but one mightier than I cometh, the latchet of whose shoes I am not worthy to unloose: he shall baptize you with the Holy Ghost and with fire: Now when all the people were baptized, it came to pass, that Jesus also being baptized, and praying, the heaven was opened, And the Holy Ghost descended in a bodily shape like a dove upon him, and a voice came from heaven, which said, Thou art my beloved Son; in thee I am well pleased. (Luke 3:1–4, 15, 16, 21, 22)

Our Lord's first Passover was on April 19, 29 AD and His fourth and last Passover was on April 10, 32 AD. The following chart will list the date conversions from the Jewish calendar to our Roman calendar:

Day	32 A.D. Hebrew	32 A.D. Roman	Event
Sunday	Nisan 10	April 6	Trumphal Entry
Monday	Nisan 11	April 7	Three Days Observation Exodus 12:3, 6
Tuesday	Nisan 12	April 8	Meal in Bethany Jesus Annointed for Burial
Wednesday	Nisan 13	April 9	Last Supper - Betrayal Preparation - Passover
Thursday	Nisan 14	April 10	Passover - Sabbath Crucifixion 9 A.M. to 3 P.M. - Burial Before Dark Preparation - Feast of Unleaven Bread Day 1
Friday	Nisan 15	April 11	Feast of Unleaven Bread - Sabbath Preparation - Weekly Sabbath Day 2 and Night 1
Saturday	Nisan 16	April 12	Weekly Sabbath Day 3 and Night 2
Sunday	Nisan 17	April 13	Resurrection before Dawn Night 3

100

To calculate from another angle, we know that from 445 BC to 32 AD is 476 full years, so 476 x 365 = 173,740 days + 118 days for leap years + 22 days from March 14 to April 6 = 173,880 days!

Calendar for year 32 (Israel)

January	February	March
Su Mo Tu We Th Fr Sa	Su Mo Tu We Th Fr Sa	Su Mo Tu We Th Fr Sa
1 2 3 4 5	1 2	1
6 7 8 9 10 11 12	3 4 5 6 7 8 9	2 3 4 5 6 7 8
13 14 15 16 17 18 19	10 11 12 13 14 15 16	9 10 11 12 13 14 15
20 21 22 23 24 25 26	17 18 19 20 21 22 23	16 17 18 19 20 21 22
27 28 29 30 31	24 25 26 27 28 29	23 24 25 26 27 28 29
		30 31
1:● 8:◐ 16:○ 24:◑ 31:●	7:◐ 15:○ 22:◑ 29:●	7:◐ 15:○ 23:◑ 29:●

April	May	June
Su Mo Tu We Th Fr Sa	Su Mo Tu We Th Fr Sa	Su Mo Tu We Th Fr Sa
1 2 3 4 5	1 2 3	1 2 3 4 5 6 7
6 7 8 9 10 11 12	4 5 6 7 8 9 10	8 9 10 11 12 13 14
13 14 15 16 17 18 19	11 12 13 14 15 16 17	15 16 17 18 19 20 21
20 21 22 23 24 25 26	18 19 20 21 22 23 24	22 23 24 25 26 27 28
27 28 29 30	25 26 27 28 29 30 31	29 30
6:◐ 14:○ 21:◑ 28:●	6:◐ 13:○ 20:◑ 27:●	5:◐ 12:○ 18:◑ 26:●

From the triumphal entry on April 6 (Nisan 10), 32 AD, there needed to be three days of observation of the sacrificial lamb, which we now know was to be the Lord Jesus Christ, when He was crucified on Thursday, April 10 (Nisan 14), 32 AD.

> Speak ye unto all the congregation of Israel, saying, In the tenth day of this month they shall take to them every man a lamb, according to the house of their fathers, a lamb for an house: And if the household be too little for the lamb, let him and his neighbour next unto his house take it according to the number of the souls; every man according to his eating shall make your count for the lamb. Your lamb shall be without blemish, a male of the

first year: ye shall take it out from the sheep, or from the goats: And ye shall keep it up until the fourteenth day of the same month: and the whole assembly of the congregation of Israel shall kill it in the evening. (Exodus 12:3–6)

Let us pause at this point and look at another option that was available to the Jews, if they all would have believed in Jesus Christ as Messiah, as He rode into Jerusalem on that Sunday. I have heard it asked from time to time, "What would have happened if Israel would have believed in her Messiah and did not crucify Him during this time? Would there have been no sacrifice for our sins and no hope of salvation?" According to Psalm 118:26–27, God's plan involved Jesus Christ being sacrificed on the altar at this time based on this prophecy: "Blessed be he that cometh in the name of the LORD: we have blessed you out of the house of the LORD. God is the LORD, which hath shewed us light: *bind the sacrifice with cords, even unto the horns of the altar*" (Psalm 118:26–27).

The partial fulfillment is recorded in all four gospels:

And the multitudes that went before, and that followed, cried, saying, Hosanna to the Son of David: Blessed is he that cometh in the name of the Lord; Hosanna in the highest. (Matthew 21:9)

And they that went before, and they that followed, cried, saying, Hosanna; Blessed is he that cometh in the name of the Lord. (Mark 11:9)

Saying, Blessed be the King that cometh in the name of the Lord: peace in heaven, and glory in the highest. (Luke 19:38)

Took branches of palm trees, and went forth to meet him,

and cried, Hosanna: Blessed is the King of Israel that cometh in the name of the Lord. (John 12:13)

Due to the unbelief of the majority in Israel, especially among her leaders, they failed to complete the fulfillment of this prophecy, when they did not "*bind the sacrifice with cords, even unto the horns of the altar.*"

God's Plan of Salvation Not Thwarted by Unbelief

So, had the entire nation of Israel accepted her Messiah, as He rode into Jerusalem on Sunday morning, April 6, 32 AD (Nisan 10, 32 AD), we refer to as the triumphal entry or Palm Sunday, the Jewish High Priest should have known exactly what needed to be done. He was to "bind the sacrifice with cords, even unto the horns of the altar." This would have provided the once and for all sacrifice to pay for the sins of all believing mankind past, present, and future. But due to unbelief they knew nothing of this, and as a result, God allowed the "sacrifice" to take place, in their unbelief on the cross, four days later on the Passover that occurred on Thursday, April 10, 32 AD (Nisan 14, 32 AD).

God Begins a New Program Called the "Mystery"

The apostle Peter preached the "bad news of the cross" fifty days later at Pentecost, Monday June 9, 32 AD when he said, "Ye have taken, and by wicked hands have crucified and slain" (Acts 2:23). It was not until a year later, after the stoning of Stephen, that the apostle Paul was raised up to proclaim the "good news of the cross." This is the "gospel of the grace of God" and Paul was to offer it to Jews and Gentiles alike in the program given to him known as the "mystery." It was a mystery because it was not forecast in the Old

Testament, and for good reason. "For had they known it (the mystery), they would not have crucified the Lord of glory" (I Corinthians 2:8). God, by keeping this mystery "hid in Him" (Ephesians 3:9), completely caught His enemies—both physical (Jewish leadership) and spiritual (Satan and his fallen angels) off guard and made it possible for anyone, thereafter, to have salvation, with their sins paid for, by simply believing that the Lord Jesus Christ died for their sins, was buried, and rose again the third day (Sunday, April 13, 32 AD).

A year later, after the stoning of Stephen in 33 AD, God set aside the chosen nation Israel in unbelief and through the apostle Paul offered salvation to all mankind in a new joint (Jew and Gentile) body known as the body of Christ. The Lord Jesus Christ began to appear to the apostle Paul by direct heavenly visions and revelations, and over about the next thirty years made known the details of the new mystery program. Paul recorded all he received from the Lord in his thirteen epistles (Romans through Philemon). "It is not expedient for me doubtless to glory. I will come to visions and revelations of the Lord" (II Corinthians 12:1).

Just as the Jews failed to recognize that God changed their program in 33 AD, today, we have over 400 denominations that differ based on which parts of the previous kingdom program are improperly mixed with the new mystery program. Today, we do not dare add anything from the old program onto the sacrifice provided by Christ on the cross, "lest the cross of Christ should be made of none effect" (I Corinthians 1:17). The cross is all-sufficient and there is nothing we can do to help earn our salvation. The only response that matters to God is that we have believing faith in the gospel of His grace. Many people believe that we have to do our little part. Yes, that is somewhat true, but if our little part is more than believing that Christ died for our sins, was buried, and rose again the third day, it is unnecessary, unwanted by God, and could well make the cross of Christ of none effect.

With the crucifixion on Thursday, we now have solved the question we started with, as to the fulfillment of the three days and three nights: Thursday being Day 1, Friday being Night 1 and Day 2, Saturday being Night 2 and Day 3, and Sunday being Night 3. The Jewish day started at 6:00 p.m. and we know that our Lord arose before dawn on Sunday the 13th.

Most of the confusion surrounding this question concerns the use of the terms "sabbath" and "preparation," especially in the book of John.

"The Jews therefore, because it was the preparation, that the bodies should not remain upon the cross on the sabbath day, (for that sabbath day was an high day,) besought Pilate that their legs might be broken, and that they might be taken away" (John 19:31).

According to the Jewish custom, there were three sabbaths and three preparations. The day before the weekly sabbath (Nisan 16/April 12) was a preparation day and the day before the Passover (Nisan 14/April 10) and the feast of unleavened bread (Nisan 15/April 11) were preparation days as well. In the verse above John says, "that sabbath day was an high day," meaning that it was the Passover sabbath as well as the preparation day for the feast of unleavened bread (which also was a sabbath). As you can see from the chart on page 100, there were three preparation days and three sabbaths in a row from April 9th through April 12th.

I do not know how the critics are going to explain this one. One thing you may run into, when you try to share these wonderful truths, is someone saying, "Well, you know you can always prove anything with the Bible, but I don't trust it because it could have been made up just to look like that." The most difficult objection to overcome is when someone doubts the inerrancy and veracity of the Word of God. (May God help us to reach them!)

CHAPTER 14

Our Relationship
with Christ

O ur relationship with Christ today is based on a different set of circumstances than those of the Christians
at the time of Christ, early in the first century. Then, the
relationship was based on actually seeing Christ, and
hearing Him teach personally, and through the twelve
apostles. From the passage in Acts 2:17–20, we know that
if the Jewish nation had responded to the gospel of the
kingdom, that the day of the Lord would have eventually
occurred that would have paved the way for the actual
"kingdom of heaven" to be brought to the earth from
heaven by Christ Himself. There, He would have reigned
from the throne of David, and the twelve apostles would
have sat on twelve thrones judging the twelve tribes of
the nation Israel. The first phase of this eternal kingdom
we now know is to be 1,000 years.

> And it shall come to pass in the last days, saith God,
> I will pour out of my Spirit upon all flesh: and your sons
> and your daughters shall prophesy, and your young men
> shall see visions, and your old men shall dream dreams:
> And on my servants and on my handmaidens I will pour

out in those days of my Spirit; and they shall prophesy.

(Intermission of Grace)

And I will shew wonders in heaven above, and signs in the earth beneath; blood, and fire, and vapour of smoke: The sun shall be turned into darkness, and the moon into blood, before that great and notable day of the Lord come. (Acts 2:17–20)

In Peter's next address/sermon, the actual offer of the kingdom, if the nation Israel would repent and be converted, is recorded: "Repent ye therefore, and be converted, that your sins may be blotted out, when the times of refreshing shall come from the presence of the Lord; And he shall send Jesus Christ, which before was preached unto you: Whom the heaven must receive until the times of restitution of all things, which God hath spoken by the mouth of all his holy prophets since the world began" (Acts 3:19–21).

When most of the nation Israel, especially among her leaders, did not respond to the gospel of the kingdom (i.e., bear fruit), the extra year was granted from the parable in Luke 13:

He spake also this parable; A certain man had a fig tree planted in his vineyard; and he came and sought fruit thereon, and found none. Then said he unto the dresser of his vineyard, Behold, these three years I come seeking fruit on this fig tree, and find none: cut it down; why cumbereth it the ground? And he answering said unto him, Lord, let it alone this year also, till I shall dig about it, and dung it: And if it *bear fruit*, well: and if not, then after that thou shalt cut it down. (Luke 13:6–9)

During the extra year not only was insufficient fruit produced, but also the persecution of the few Christians began to ramp up.

We know from the first census of Israel (Numbers 1:21–47) at the time of Moses, in about 1,490 BC, that the population of Israel was 603,550 for males age 20 and above, not including the tribe of Levi. An estimate for the population of Israel, at the time of Christ, is 3,000,000. The book of Acts records that 3,000 plus 5,000 men were saved on the day of Pentecost and shortly thereafter: "Then they that gladly received his word were baptized: and the same day there were added unto them about three thousand souls" (Acts 2:41). "Howbeit many of them which heard the word believed; and the number of the men was about five thousand" (Acts 4:4).

The relationship these Christians had with Christ was based on them knowing Him firsthand and through His apostles, who had been with Him during His three-year earthly ministry.

If the nation Israel would have responded to the kingdom gospel, the seventieth week of Daniel would have begun, after an indeterminant period of time, and that seven years of tribulation would have resulted in the battle of Armageddon followed by the establishment of the one thousand-year kingdom reign of Christ on earth.

The relationship of these saints would also have been based on seeing Christ Himself and hearing Him as He reigned from David's throne.

When Israel did not respond and the extra year expired, God in matchless grace, struck down the chief persecutor of the Christians. Then He saved him (Saul of Tarsus, also known as Paul), commissioned him an apostle, and sent him forth with a new gospel of the grace of God. The difference in this gospel is that you are saved by Christ's blood and His blood alone by believing that He died for your sins, was buried, and rose again on the third day.

This whole program is called the mystery and is outlined in Paul's thirteen epistles that he penned, through the guidance of the Holy Spirit, as he was receiving direct heavenly revelations from Jesus Christ Himself, over about a thirty-year period.

Our relationship with Christ today, during this time of the outpouring of God's grace, is not based on knowing Him in a physical presence, but through the Holy Spirit and the inspired Word that was written primarily through the apostle Paul. At the moment we believe, we are baptized into (or identified with) the body of Christ by the Holy Spirit. "For by one Spirit are we all baptized into one body, whether we be Jews or Gentiles, whether we be bond or free; and have been all made to drink into one Spirit" (I Corinthians 12:13). This has nothing to with the water ceremony (known as baptism) that would have prepared the nation of Israel to become that "kingdom of priests," had they not rejected the kingdom gospel, as recorded so clearly in the first 8 chapters of the book of Acts.

Sometimes our preachers today try to get us to think about having the kind of relationship with Christ that the kingdom saints had during the early Acts period. This can make sense to them because they unwittingly mix some of the interrupted kingdom gospel into today's message of reconciliation through the gospel of the grace of God. In order to understand what God has so clearly communicated to us today, we must rightly divide the Word of truth so that we do not get a confusing mixture. This has always been true, down through the ages, as God has changed His dealing with mankind numerous times, due to sin, rebellion, rejection, and unbelief.

Not understanding our proper relationship with Christ today can cause many to question whether they

are even saved, because they do not seem to have the same emotional relationship that others profess to have with Christ. Paul was inspired to write in II Corinthians 5:16, "Wherefore henceforth know we no man after the flesh: yea, though we have known Christ after the flesh, yet now henceforth know we him no more."

Today, we know Christ and have a relationship with Him through the Holy Spirit, as we study the Words of Christ recorded in Paul's epistles, e.g.: "Since ye seek a proof of Christ speaking in me, which to you-ward is not weak, but is mighty in you" (II Corinthians 13:3).

Our program today is extremely good news to a lost and dying world, and the best thing about it is that it is, by far, God's best and simplest program to date. For that reason, it is the enemy's (Satan's) worst nightmare. He will try anything to stop it through confusion and misunderstanding. Down through the ages he has used primarily other Christians in this effort. It started with the Judaizers who tried to mix in circumcision and the Law of Moses with the grace gospel Paul had shared with the Gentiles in Antioch. (See the book of Galatians.) The apostle Paul was given what he called "my gospel, and the preaching of Jesus Christ according to the revelation of the mystery, which was kept secret since the world began" (Romans 16:25), and that made him an enemy of anyone who fails to see the Intermission of Grace. Satan sees it but is trying to do anything he can to discredit the message. It was tough sledding for Paul because we know that by the time he was finishing his ministry, all in Asia had turned away from him and his inspired message: "This thou knowest, that all they which are in Asia be turned away from me; of whom are Phygellus and Hermogenes" (II Timothy 1:15).

As we lost the importance of the distinctive apostleship of Paul, the Christian community was plunged into a period of confusion that is still prevalent today. During the 1500s the Reformation began by recovering the truth of "faith alone in Christ alone." During the 1800s the truth of the rapture was recovered along with the difference between Israel and the church, the body of Christ. Finally, during the 1930s, the truth of the distinctive message and ministry of the apostle Paul began to be recovered. It is still Satan's worst nightmare, today, and is still under massive attacks from all sides.

During the last few hundred years, we have seen the establishment of most of the modern schools of thought, pertaining to the understanding of Scripture. As a result, much of what we are being taught today is not based on God's clear message for us from Scripture, but on an improper mixture of His various programs that have become "tradition of men" and "rudiments of the world." "Beware lest any man spoil you through philosophy and vain deceit, after the tradition of men, after the rudiments of the world, and not after Christ" (Colossians 2:8). "Howbeit in vain do they worship me, teaching for doctrines the commandments of men. Making the word of God of none effect through your tradition, which ye have delivered: and many such like things do ye" (Mark 7:7, 13).

Many Christians are in substantial bondage today because they haven't been exposed to the "simplicity that is in Christ" from the gospel of the grace of God, and that His blood and His blood alone can save you if you simply believe that He died for your sins, was buried, and rose again the third day: "But I fear, lest by any means, as the serpent beguiled Eve through his subtilty, so your minds should be corrupted from the simplicity that is in Christ" (II Corinthians 11:3).

I have interviewed numerous Protestant pastors over the last few years and have asked them, "Just exactly what does one need to do today to be saved?" The list I have compiled is a long one. Among the things on the list are repent, make Him Lord of your life, confess your sins, ask Him into your heart, have a personal relationship with Him, obey His commandments, go to church, be water baptized—and the list goes on.

You can boil the gospel of the grace of God down to one word: believe. That is the only response God requires for us to appropriate the gift of salvation, provided by the blood of the Lord Jesus Christ upon the cross. Anything we try to add on to this believing faith is unnecessary and unwanted by God. Naturally, your behavior and works will show evidence that you are saved, but you are not saved by good works. You have good works because you are saved.

Just try to solve the following seeming contradiction in Scripture, if you do not rightly divide the Word of God into its separate programs.

> Ye see then how that by works a man is justified, and not by faith only. (James 2:24)

> Therefore we conclude that a man is justified by faith without the deeds of the law. (Romans 3:28)

> But to him that worketh not, but believeth on him that justifieth the ungodly, his faith is counted for righteousness. (Romans 4:5)

There was a time when God required works and deeds as evidence of faith. During the kingdom gospel, water baptism was required for salvation. "He that believeth and is baptized shall be saved; but he that believeth not shall be damned" (Mark 16:16).

Another seeming contradiction in Scripture will demonstrate that God has changed His program for dealing with us about forgiving.

> For if ye forgive men their trespasses, your heavenly Father will also forgive you: But if ye forgive not men their trespasses, neither will your Father forgive (present tense) your trespasses. (Mathew 6:14–15)

> And be ye kind one to another, tenderhearted, forgiving one another, even as God for Christ's sake hath forgiven (past tense) you. (Ephesians 4:32)

> Forbearing one another, and forgiving one another, if any man have a quarrel against any: even as Christ forgave (past tense) you, so also do ye. (Colossians 3:13)

Today we are forgiven all trespasses the moment we believe. "And you, being dead in your sins and the uncircumcision of your flesh, hath he quickened together with him, having forgiven you all trespasses" (Colossians 2:13).

Today, thankfully, we are saved simply by believing and having faith in the finished work of Christ on the cross, when He paid the price once for all the sins of believing mankind past, present, and future. Today, you can know that you are eternally saved by believing the gospel that Christ died for your sins, was buried, and rose again the third day. "Moreover, brethren, I declare unto you the gospel which I preached unto you, which also ye have received, and wherein ye stand; By which also ye are saved, if ye keep in memory what I preached unto you, unless ye have believed in vain. For I delivered unto you first of all that which I also received, how that Christ died for our sins according to the scriptures; And that he was buried, and that he rose again the third day according to the scriptures" (I Corinthians 15:1–4).

Couple the last verses with these next two passages, and you will know all you need to know about how to be saved, and what to tell others about how they can be saved, as well. "For by grace are ye saved through faith; and that not of yourselves: it is the gift of God: Not of works, lest any man should boast. For we are his workmanship, created in Christ Jesus unto good works, which God hath before ordained that we should walk in them" (Ephesians 2:8–10).

Notice, that it is grace that saves you, that you appropriate through faith (believing). It is the gift of God and has nothing to do with works or deeds. A lot of people get tricked into thinking, "but we have to do our little part." That is somewhat true but if "our little part" is anything more than believing faith, it is contrary to Scripture. "Not by works of righteousness which we have done, but according to his mercy he saved us, by the washing of regeneration, and renewing of the Holy Ghost; Which he shed on us abundantly through Jesus Christ our Saviour; That being justified by his grace, we should be made heirs according to the hope of eternal life. This is a faithful saying, and these things I will that thou affirm constantly, that they which have believed in God might be careful to maintain good works. These things are good and profitable unto men" (Titus 3:5–8).

Although not required for salvation, works are "ordained (prepared) that we should walk in them" and be "careful to maintain" because they are "good and profitable." One clear teaching of Scripture is that because of sin, our righteous acts are not worth much. "But we are all as an unclean thing, and all our righteousnesses are as filthy rags; and we all do fade as a leaf; and our iniquities, like the wind, have taken us away" (Isaiah 64:6).

When we feel we must do something more than believe the gospel, we are demonstrating that we do not have faith that Christ's blood shed on the cross was powerful enough to completely pay for all our sins and make it possible to be reconciled to God. Being that our salvation is a gift from a loving God, there is nothing that we could ever do that would be remotely good enough to be worth anything compared to God's grace. Praise God!

How can you have the assurance, that what you have just read is true, based on the Word of God? If you have believed the gospel and are indwelt by the Holy Spirit, the only way is to:

Study—Rightly Divide—Search—Reread

"*Study* to shew thyself approved unto God, a workman that needeth not to be ashamed, *rightly dividing* the word of truth" (II Timothy 2:15). "And the brethren immediately sent away Paul and Silas by night unto Berea: who coming thither went into the synagogue of the Jews. These were more noble than those in Thessalonica, in that they received the word with all readiness of mind, and *searched* the scriptures daily, whether those things were so" (Acts 17:10–11).

François Mauriac: "If you would tell me the heart of a man, tell me not what he reads but what he *rereads*."

I have heard it said, "Read a lot, but not too many books," and I have personally observed people that have been misled by exposing themselves to false doctrine in books that try to refute truth contained in the Scriptures. If you do not stray too far from the Word of God, you will be insulated from false doctrine. An analogy comes from the banking industry. Bankers are trained to spot and detect counterfeit currency, and the primary tool is to be acutely familiar with the real thing. Once you thoroughly learn how real money feels, a counterfeit bill will stick out like a sore thumb. By the same token, once you have studied, rightly divided, searched, and reread the truth sufficiently, you can spot and detect false doctrine quickly. This is where the Holy Spirit comes in and will assist you in not being misled by false doctrine. Just like the bankers, this will require patience, effort, and diligence, but it will be well worth the time required, when you consider what a disaster it would be to be fooled by counterfeit money or false doctrine.

"That we henceforth be no more children, tossed to and fro, and carried about with every wind of doctrine, by the sleight of men, and cunning craftiness, whereby they lie in wait to deceive" (Ephesians 4:14).

By following the above, you will be able to begin to be led by the Spirit and will start to display the fruit of the Spirit as listed for us in the book of Galatians. "But the fruit of the Spirit is love, joy, peace, longsuffering, gentleness, goodness, faith, Meekness, temperance: against such there is no law" (Galatians 5:22–23).

If you really study the Scriptures (especially Paul's letters), you will be taught by the Spirit all you need to know concerning having a right relationship with Christ. The first thing you will experience is gratitude for what He has done for you on the cross. It is understandable that then and only then will you feel confident to share this glorious message with others as the Spirit leads you. God knows that it is not His harshness but His goodness that compels us to be repentant and render service to Him. "Or despisest thou the riches of his goodness and forbearance and longsuffering; not knowing that the goodness of God leadeth thee to repentance?" (Romans 2:4)

117

Again, the other thing we need to watch for is improper influence from even well-meaning friends, relatives, or preachers who would corrupt the "simplicity that is in Christ" and the message of salvation, based on His finished work on the cross, by adding anything on to grace, and therefore making the cross of Christ of none effect. "But I fear, lest by any means, as the serpent beguiled Eve through his subtilty, so your minds should be corrupted from the simplicity that is in Christ" (II Corinthians 11:3). "For Christ sent me not to baptize, but to preach the gospel: not with wisdom of words, lest the cross of Christ should be made of none effect" (I Corinthians 1:17).

When we improperly mix the various programs of God, we introduce confusion and uncertainty that makes it difficult for the unsaved to hear and respond to the clear message of salvation. "For if the trumpet give an uncertain sound, who shall prepare himself to the battle?" (I Corinthians 14:8)

Sometimes grace believers, who rightly divide the Scriptures, are accused of being "Bible choppers" and not valuing Scriptures other than the apostle Paul's letters. This is an unfair accusation because, based on Scripture, the whole Bible is profitable and inspired by the Holy Spirit, and for anyone to not value the whole Bible would be unwise. "All scripture *is* given by inspiration of God, and *is* profitable for doctrine, for reproof, for correction, for instruction in righteousness: That the man of God may be perfect, thoroughly furnished unto all good works" (II Timothy 3:16). "For the prophecy came not in old time by the will of man: but holy men of God spake as they were moved by the Holy Ghost" (II Peter 1:21).

CHAPTER 15

Everlasting Life Assurance Policy
(Print this to share)

U pon satisfaction of the terms of this contract, the
owner is given, by the Spirit, the assurance of everlasting life with God the Father, God the Son, and God
the Holy Spirit.

Date: _____

Issued to: _____

The undersigned hereby serves as witness that the
terms of this contract have been satisfied:

Witness: _____

The Risk–Peril
Sin has separated us from God and, if we face, in our
unresolved sinful state, His condemnation and judgment,
we are doomed to hell for eternity in the lake of fire,
without God.

For all have sinned, and come short of the glory of God. (Romans 3:23)

Wherefore, as by one man sin entered into the world, and death by sin; and so death passed upon all men, for that all have sinned. (Romans 5:12)

For the wages of sin is death; but the gift of God is eternal life through Jesus Christ our Lord. (Romans 6:23)

And death and hell were cast into the lake of fire. This is the second death. And whosoever was not found written in the book of life was cast into the lake of fire. (Revelation 20:14–15)

The Coverage

God has provided a method whereby you can have coverage for your sins. This coverage was provided through the sacrifice of His Son, the Lord Jesus Christ, whose shed blood, and death on the cross serves as payment for all your past, present, and future sins. Christ died your death on the cross and shed His blood for your sins.

That if thou shalt confess with thy mouth the Lord Jesus, and shalt believe in thine heart that God hath raised him from the dead, thou shalt be saved. For with the heart man believeth unto righteousness; and with the mouth confession is made unto salvation. For the scripture saith, Whosoever believeth on him shall not be ashamed. For there is no difference between the Jew and the Greek: for the same Lord over all is rich unto all that call upon him. For whosoever shall call upon the name of the Lord shall be saved. (Romans 10:9–13)

Moreover, brethren, I declare unto you the gospel which I preached unto you, which also ye have received, and wherein ye stand; By which also ye are saved, if ye keep in memory what I preached unto you, unless ye have believed in vain. For I delivered unto you first of all that which I also received, how that Christ died for our sins according to the scriptures; And that he was buried, and that he rose again the third day according to the scriptures. (I Corinthians 15:1–4)

For by grace are ye saved through faith; and that not of yourselves: it is the gift of God: Not of works, lest any man should boast. (Ephesians 2:8–9)

When you believe that Christ died for your sins, was buried, and rose again the third day, based on the above Scriptures, with all your heart, the Holy Spirit immediately baptizes you into (or identifies you with) the body of Christ and into His death. "For by one Spirit are we all baptized into one body, whether we be Jews or Gentiles, whether we be bond or free; and have been all made to drink into one Spirit" (I Corinthians 12:13). "Know ye not, that so many of us as were baptized into Jesus Christ were baptized into his death?" (Romans 6:3)

Once you are saved, you are sealed forever and become a member of a new creature/creation in Christ, and God sees you in Christ, seated at His right hand, in heavenly places.

In whom ye also trusted, after that ye heard the word of truth, the gospel of your salvation: in whom also after that ye believed, ye were sealed with that holy Spirit of promise. (Ephesians 1:13)

And grieve not the holy Spirit of God, whereby ye are sealed unto the day of redemption. (Ephesians 4:30)

Therefore if any man be in Christ, he is a new creature: old things are passed away; behold, all things are become new. (I Corinthians 5:17)

And hath raised us up together, and made us sit together in heavenly places in Christ Jesus. (Ephesians 2:6)

What the Bible Teaches about Your Future if You are Saved

If you die before the Lord returns in the rapture, your soul and spirit will immediately be with the Lord: "Therefore we are always confident, knowing that, whilst we are at home in the body, we are absent from the Lord: (For we walk by faith, not by sight:) We are confident, I say, and willing rather to be absent from the body, and to be present with the Lord" (II Corinthians 5:6–8). "For I am in a strait betwixt two, having a desire to depart, and to be with Christ; which is far better: Nevertheless to abide in the flesh is more needful for you" (Philippians 1:23–24).

Your body will be resurrected and changed to perfection when the Lord returns in the air to take you to heaven:

> Behold, I shew you a mystery; We shall not all sleep, but we shall all be changed, In a moment, in the twinkling of an eye, at the last trump: for the trumpet shall sound, and the dead shall be raised incorruptible, and we shall be changed. For this corruptible must put on incorruption, and this mortal must put on immortality. (I Corinthians 15:51–53)

> For if we believe that Jesus died and rose again, even so them also which sleep in Jesus will God bring with him. For this we say unto you by the word of the Lord, that we which are alive and remain unto the coming of the Lord shall not prevent them which are asleep. For the Lord himself shall descend from heaven with a shout, with the voice of the archangel, and with the trump of God: and the dead in Christ shall rise first: Then we which are alive and remain shall be caught up together with them in the clouds, to meet the Lord in the air: and so shall we ever be with the Lord. Wherefore comfort one another with these words. (I Thessalonians 4:14–18)

If you are alive at the Lord's return, you are await-ing the Lord's return at the rapture. "Looking for that blessed hope, and the glorious appearing of the great God and our Savior Jesus Christ" (Titus 2:13). "Now we beseech you, brethren, by the coming of our Lord Jesus Christ, and by our gathering together unto him" (II Thessalonians 2:1).

You will be taken off the earth and given a new body as you meet the Lord in the air: I Corinthians 15:51–53 and I Thessalonians 4:14–17. (See above.)

You will spend eternity with God the Father, the Lord Jesus Christ, and the Holy Spirit in a perfect and sinless state. "That in the ages to come he might shew the exceeding riches of his grace in his kindness toward us through Christ Jesus" (Ephesians 2:7).

What the Bible Teaches about Your Future if You are Not Saved

If you are not saved and die before the Lord returns in the rapture, your soul and spirit will immediately be in hell, and your body will be raised on the last day to face the White Throne Judgment:

> And it came to pass, that the beggar died, and was carried by the angels into Abraham's bosom: the rich man also died, and was buried; And in hell he lift up his eyes, being in torments, and seeth Abraham afar off, and Lazarus in his bosom. And he cried and said, Father Abraham, have mercy on me, and send Lazarus, that he may dip the tip of his finger in water, and cool my tongue; for I am tormented in this flame. (Luke 16:22–24)

> For if God spared not the angels that sinned, but cast them down to hell, and delivered them into chains of darkness, to be reserved unto judgment; The Lord knoweth how to deliver the godly out of temptations, and to reserve

the unjust unto the day of judgment to be punished.
(II Peter 2:4, 9)

And I saw a great white throne, and him that sat on it,
from whose face the earth and the heaven fled away;
and there was found no place for them. And I saw the
dead, small and great, stand before God; and the books
were opened: and another book was opened, which is
the book of life: and the dead were judged out of those
things which were written in the books, according to
their works. (Revelation 20:11–12)

If you are not saved and alive at the Lord's return in
the rapture, you will go into the seven years of tribulation
and wrath with none of the saved left on the earth.

For then shall be great tribulation, such as was not since
the beginning of the world to this time, no, nor ever shall
be. (Matthew 24:21)

But after thy hardness and impenitent heart treasurest up
unto thyself wrath against the day of wrath and revelation
of the righteous judgment of God. (Romans 2:5)

Let no man deceive you with vain words: for because of
these things cometh the wrath of God upon the children
of disobedience. (Ephesians 5:6)

And said to the mountains and rocks, Fall on us, and
hide us from the face of him that sitteth on the throne,
and from the wrath of the Lamb: For the great day
of his wrath is come; and who shall be able to stand?
(Revelation 6:16–17)

To become saved during the seven-year tribulation
will be difficult, at best, and would most likely result in
your being martyred. "And when he had opened the fifth
seal, I saw under the altar the souls of them that were
slain for the word of God, and for the testimony which
they held" (Revelation 6:9). "And I said unto him, Sir,

thou knowest. And he said to me, These are they which came out of great tribulation, and have washed their robes, and made them white in the blood of the Lamb" (Revelation 7:14).

If you die during the seven-year tribulation, without being saved, or reject Christ and are alive at the end of the seven years, you will spend eternity, without God, tormented in the lake of fire. "And death and hell were cast into the lake of fire. This is the second death. And whosoever was not found written in the book of life was cast into the lake of fire" (Revelation 20:14–15).

> Dear Heavenly Father,
> I confess that I am a sinner and helpless to find a way to pay for my sins, to be reconciled unto You. I thank You for Your offer of salvation and the forgiveness of my sins as a free gift of Your grace. I believe that Your Son, the Lord Jesus Christ, died for my sins, was buried, and rose again the third day, and that His death, burial, and resurrection fully paid the price for all my sins. He died the death that I deserve, and You accept His death for the payment of all my sins, and for that I will be eternally grateful. I thank You, praise You, and give You all the glory, honor, and adoration. It is in the precious name of the Lord Jesus Christ that I pray, with thanksgiving, Amen.

Remember, if Christianity turns out to be a hoax, you will be no worse off for having truly believed this gospel of the grace of God. If, however, Christianity turns out to be true, this will be, by far, the most important decision you make in this life, so do not delay for "behold, now is the accepted time; behold, now is the day of salvation" (II Corinthians 6:2).

The chart below diagrams and illustrates the Biblical progression of life from where we are now.

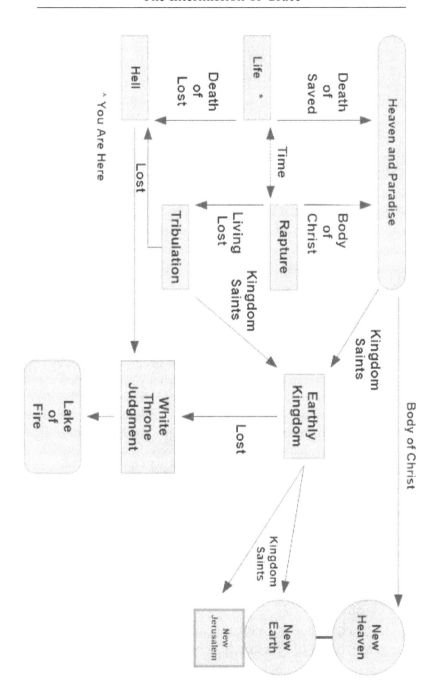

CHAPTER 16

The Dimension of Love

In this author's first book, *Understanding the Bible and End Times*, in footnote 7 on page 71, the dimension of love was described as "the pinnacle" to be dealt with, in detail, in this Book Two. This chapter will endeavor to do just that.

In I Corinthians 13 after explaining that the gifts of the Spirit would no longer be needed after "that which is perfect is come," vs. 10, meaning the completed Word of God, Paul goes on to say that the gifts would be "done away." In verse 13 he ends by stating that "now abideth (Greek, *meno*—remain) faith, hope, charity (love—Greek, *agapi*), these three; but the greatest of these is charity (love)."

God's primary quality is love, and this is demonstrated throughout the Bible. The greatest demonstration of His love was the sacrifice of His Son on the cross to pay for all our sins. He wants us to be with Him for all eternity as His sons and daughters, that He is conforming to the image of His Son. This is prominently depicted in Romans 8:28–29. "And we know that all things work together for good to them that love God, to them who are the called according to his purpose. For whom he did foreknow, he also did predestinate to be conformed to the image of his Son, that he might be the firstborn among many brethren."

These verses can be uplifting at times, but generally the body of Christ does not know the best part of them. Let us take a closer look.

We see in the first phrase, "we know that all things work together for good"—a statement of fact, for the Greek word translated "know" refers to something that has been established beyond doubt or something that is sure and a certainty. No equivocation there. We also see that the statement is all-inclusive, for the words "all things" exclude nothing. However, the question that immediately arises relates to the use of the word "good," for it requires a value judgment. After all, that which many consider to be good may not be considered good by you at all. Since there is only one value judgment that is at all relevant, namely the judgment of God, we know that this question can only be answered with reference to what God considers to be good.

When we move on in the text of Romans 8:28, we see the definition of the class to which the statement applies which is, "them that love God," which in this context of Scripture, refers to the Christian, for we cannot know, let alone love, God except through Jesus Christ. (See John 14:6–7.) Following this definition of the class, there is another class definition in the phrase, "to them who are the called according to His purpose." This phrase refers to the Christian as well, for the Greek word translated "the called" also means "the invited," "the appointed," and "a saint." While we see that the statement in verse 28 applies to the Christian as a person, who loves God, and is one of "the called" according to God's purpose, the definition of that purpose is not supplied. However, the question of what is good is answered, for anything that advances God's purpose is, by definition, good, and anything that hinders God's purpose is, by definition, bad. Therefore, we know that everything (though hard to believe at times) that happens in the world to the believer works to advance God's purpose regarding the believer.

At this point, the glaring missing piece in all this is God's purpose. When we move on to verse 29, we begin to catch a glimpse of what God's purpose is, as it reads, "For whom He did foreknow, He also did predestinate to be conformed to the image of his Son, that He might be the firstborn among many brethren." However, in coming across the words "foreknow" and "predestinate," many people have been led to believe that we do not have any free will in the matter. Such is simply not the case. The Greek word translated "foreknow" simply means "to have knowledge beforehand," and the word translated "predestinate" simply means "to predetermine, decide beforehand." The fact that God knew, before creation, all those individuals who would respond to Him in faith, does not in any way affect each individual's free will in doing so. Simply stated, knowing is not the same as causing. In the same way, God ordaining that all those who would respond would be conformed to the image of His Son, does not affect the individual's free will in that response. So, when we look at these words in proper context, we see that God knew all those who would respond to Him, in faith of their own free will, and determined that each one, who would do so, would be "conformed to the image of his Son." This represents the operation of the creation but not the purpose.

When we move to the last phrase of verse 29, we come upon the expression of God's purpose for the creation—"that He (Jesus Christ) might be the firstborn among many brethren." While this process of operation is the conforming of those who love God, the purpose or reason for the creation is to (1) give birth to many, many sons and daughters and (2) establish Jesus Christ as the preeminent Son among them. By substituting equivalent expressions, we can restate Romans 8:28–29 as follows:

And we know that all things, excluding nothing, work together for good to conform those, who are begotten of God through Jesus Christ, into the image and likeness of Jesus Christ, so that He would no longer be the only Son of God, but would rather be the firstborn and preeminent Son among many, many sons and daughters, which is God's purpose for the creation. "The Spirit itself beareth witness with our spirit, that we are the children of God: And if children, then heirs; heirs of God, and joint-heirs with Christ; if so be that we suffer with him, that we may be also glorified together. For I reckon that the sufferings of this present time are not worthy to be compared with the glory which shall be revealed in us" (Romans 8:16–18).

The promise of Romans 8:28–29 is that the moment any trial or situation you find yourself in no longer advances the conforming process and begins to hinder that process, God is committed to act on your behalf. Otherwise, all things would not work together for good. This is what it means when Scripture says that "God is faithful, who will not allow you to be tempted beyond what you are able, but with the temptation will also make the way of escape, that you may be able to bear it" (I Corinthians 10:13).

So, God's main desire and purpose for creation, and a demonstration of His love, is to have many sons and daughters to enjoy a loving family relationship with, throughout eternity. We see parallels to this principle in our own lives constantly. A person can love a pet fish, but the fish's ability to understand, appreciate, and receive that love is extremely limited, as is the range of expression or communication of love and fellowship that is open to the person. Should that same person exchange the fish for a puppy, the greater capability of the puppy as he grows up to understand, appreciate, and receive love, provides the person with a much wider and deeper range of expression and fellowship, and is therefore more satisfying to the person. However, significant limitations still exist until we move to the best parallel of all, that of a child. Though the child has a limited capacity during infancy for understanding, appreciating, and receiving the fullness of the parent's expression of love, as well as the enjoyment of fellowship, the child is most like the parent, and the promise of great potential is obvious. As the child grows up, the capacity of the child to give and receive love becomes more or less equivalent to the parent, and the fullest expression of love and fellowship becomes possible.

However, there is one catch which is extremely important in understanding the nature of man as created by God. As in anything, the value of the benefit received is often related to the risk assumed. Even though the risk of rejection and rebellion would be non-existent, God could not satisfy His desire for fellowship by creating a race of robots, who would obey Him simply because they were incapable of doing otherwise. The kind of love and fellowship God desires requires a free choice, or in other words, a free will. For this reason, forced obedience is not acceptable to God either as not being an expression of free choice. God could be satisfied only by the free choice of a person to enter into a sustained relationship of love and fellowship, from which would come obedience, as the natural expression of that love.

I want to give credit for helping this author have a deeper understanding of Romans 8:28–29 to Mark D. Caswell, J.D. in his book, *The Jesus Trap*. Some of the thoughts above are from that book.

Twelve Baptisms

1. "Moreover, brethren, I would not that ye should be ignorant, how that all our fathers were under the cloud, and all passed through the sea; And were all baptized unto Moses in the cloud and in the sea" (dry baptism for Israel; Egyptians were immersed) (I Corinthians 10:1–2).

2. "Of the doctrine of baptisms, and of laying on of hands, and of resurrection of the dead, and of eternal judgment" (Hebrews 6:2). "Which stood only in meats and drinks, and divers washings, and carnal ordinances, imposed on them until the time of reformation" (washings by the law) (Hebrews 9:10).

3. "For laying aside the commandment of God, ye hold the tradition of men, as the washing of pots and cups: and many other such like things ye do" (washings added by the Rabbis) (Mark 7:8).

4. "And he came into all the country about Jordan, preaching the baptism of repentance for the remission of sins" (Luke 3:3). "This man was instructed

in the way of the Lord; and being fervent in the spirit, he spake and taught diligently the things of the Lord, knowing only the baptism of John" (water—repentance) (Acts 18:25).

5. "But John forbad him, saying, I have need to be baptized of thee, and comest thou to me? And Jesus answering said unto him, Suffer it to be so now: for thus it becometh us to fulfil all righteousness. Then he suffered him" (water) (Matthew 3:14–15).

6. "But I have a baptism to be baptized with; and how am I straitened till it be accomplished" (Luke 12:50)! "But Jesus said unto them, Ye know not what ye ask: can ye drink of the cup that I drink of? and be baptized with the baptism that I am baptized with? And they said unto him, We can. And Jesus said unto them, Ye shall indeed drink of the cup that I drink of; and with the baptism that I am baptized withal shall ye be baptized" (dry—death) (Mark 10:38–39).

7. "Which sometime were disobedient, when once the longsuffering of God waited in the days of Noah, while the ark was a preparing, wherein few, that is, eight souls were saved by water. The like figure whereunto even baptism doth also now save us (not the putting away of the filth of the flesh, but the answer of a good conscience toward God,) by the resurrection of Jesus Christ" (dry baptism for Noah; the unsaved were immersed) (I Peter 3:20–21).

8. "And, behold, I send the promise of my Father upon you: but tarry ye in the city of Jerusalem,

134

until ye be endued with power from on high" (Luke 24:49). "And, being assembled together with them, commanded them that they should not depart from Jerusalem, but wait for the promise of the Father, which, saith he, ye have heard of me" (Acts 1:4). "For John truly baptized with water; but ye shall be baptized with the Holy Ghost not many days hence" (dry—baptism with the Holy Spirit; they had already received the Holy Spirit— John 20:22) (Acts 1:5).

9. "Else what shall they do which are baptized for the dead, if the dead rise not at all? why are they then baptized for the dead?" (dry—blood of martyrs) (I Corinthians 15:29).

10. "I indeed baptize you with water unto repentance: but he that cometh after me is mightier than I, whose shoes I am not worthy to bear: he shall baptize you with the Holy Ghost, and with fire" (dry—judgment—yet future) (Matthew 3:11).

11. "Then Peter said unto them, Repent, and be baptized every one of you in the name of Jesus Christ for the remission of sins, and ye shall receive the gift of the Holy Ghost" (Acts 2:38). "And he said unto them, Go ye into all the world, and preach the gospel to every creature. He that believeth and is baptized shall be saved; but he that believeth not shall be damned. And these signs shall follow them that believe; In my name shall they cast out devils; they shall speak with new tongues; They shall take up serpents; and if they drink any deadly thing, it shall not hurt them; they shall lay hands on the sick, and they shall

recover" (water for remission of sins—followed by miraculous signs) (Mark 16:15–18).

12. "For by one Spirit are we all baptized into one body, whether we be Jews or Gentiles, whether we be bond or free; and have been all made to drink into one Spirit" (I Corinthians 12:13). "There is one body, and one Spirit, even as ye are called in one hope of your calling; One Lord, one faith, one baptism, One God and Father of all, who is above all, and through all, and in you all" (dry baptism by the Spirit into the one body) (Ephesians 4:4–6).

APPENDIX II

Did Jesus Christ die for all the sins of all sinners, and can all be saved by believing? Some say that Christ did not die for everyone, but just those whom He and God chose to be saved. The following verses will dispel that fallacy.

> Ask, and it shall be given you; seek, and ye shall find; knock, and it shall be opened unto you: For **every** one that asketh receiveth; and he that seeketh findeth; and to him that knocketh it shall be opened. (Matthew 7:7-8)

> And he said unto them, Go ye into all the world, and preach the gospel to **every** creature. (Mark 16:15)

> As it is written in the law of the Lord, **every** male that openeth the womb shall be called holy to the Lord. (Luke 2:23)

> That was the true Light, which lighteth **every** man that cometh into the world. (John 1:9)

> For God so loved the **world** that he gave his only begotten Son, that **whosoever** believeth in him should not perish, but have everlasting life. For God sent not his Son into the world to condemn the **world**; but that the **world** through him might be saved. (John 3:16–17)

And this is the will of him that sent me, that **every** one which seeth the Son, and believeth on him, may have everlasting life: and I will raise him up at the last day. (John 6:40)

It is written in the prophets, And they shall be all taught of God. **Every** man therefore that hath heard, and hath learned of the Father, cometh unto me. (John 6:45)

And by him **all** that believe are justified from all things, from which ye could not be justified by the law of Moses. (Acts 3:39)

But in **every** nation he that feareth him, and worketh righteousness, is accepted with him. (Acts 10:35)

And the times of this ignorance God winked at; but now commandeth **all** men **every** where to repent. (Acts 17:30)

For I am not ashamed of the gospel of Christ: for it is the power of God unto salvation to **every** one that believeth; to the Jew first, and also to the Greek. (Romans 1:16)

But glory, honour, and peace, to **every** man that worketh good, to the Jew first, and also to the Gentile. (Romans 2:10)

And he received the sign of circumcision, a seal of the righteousness of the faith which he had yet being uncircumcised: that he might be the father of **all** them that believe, though they be not circumcised; that righteousness might be imputed unto them also. (Romans 4:11)

Therefore it is of faith, that it might be by grace; to the end the promise might be sure to **all** the seed; "not to that only which is of the law, but to that also which is of the faith of Abraham; who is the father of us **all**. (Romans 4:16)

Therefore as by the offence of one judgment came upon all men to condemnation; even so by the righteousness of one the free gift came upon **all** men unto justification of life. (Romans 5:18)

He that spared not his own Son, but delivered him up for us **all**, how shall he not with him also freely give us all things? (Romans 8:32)

For Christ is the end of the law for righteousness to **every** one that believeth. (Romans 10:4)

For there is no difference between the Jew and the Greek: for the same Lord over all is rich unto **all** that call upon him. For **whosoever** shall call upon the name of the Lord shall be saved. (Romans 10:12–13)

And so **all** Israel shall be saved: as it is written, There shall come out of Sion the Deliverer, and shall turn away ungodliness from Jacob. (Romans 11:26)

For God hath concluded them all in unbelief, that he might have mercy upon **all**. (Romans 11:32)

For I say, through the grace given unto me, to **every** man that is among you, not to think of himself more highly than he ought to think; but to think soberly, according as God hath dealt to **every** man the measure of faith. (Romans 12:3)

And again, Praise the Lord, **all** ye Gentiles; and laud him, **all** ye people. (Romans 15:11)

For your obedience is come abroad unto **all** men. I am glad therefore on your behalf: but yet I would have you wise unto that which is good, and simple concerning evil. (Romans 16:19)

But now is made manifest, and by the scriptures of the prophets, according to the commandment of the everlasting God, made known to **all** nations for the obedience of faith. (Romans 16:26)

Unto the church of God which is at Corinth, to them that are sanctified in Christ Jesus, called to be saints, with **all** that in every place call upon the name of Jesus Christ our Lord, both theirs and ours. (I Corinthians 1:2)

Even as I please **all** men in all things, not seeking mine own profit, but the profit of many, that they may be saved. (I Corinthians 10:33)

But I would have you know, that the head of **every** man is Christ; and the head of the woman is the man; and the head of Christ is God. (I Corinthians 11:3)

But the manifestation of the Spirit is given to **every** man to profit withal. (I Corinthians 12:7)

But all these worketh that one and the selfsame Spirit, dividing to **every** man severally as he will. (I Corinthians 12:11)

For as in Adam all die, even so in Christ shall **all** be made alive. (I Corinthians 15:22)

And when all things shall be subdued unto him, then shall the Son also himself be subject unto him that put all things under him, that God may be all in **all**. (I Corinthians 15:28)

For the love of Christ constraineth us; because we thus judge, that if one died for **all**, then were all dead. (II Corinthians 5:14)

And that he died for **all**, that they which live should not henceforth live unto themselves, but unto him which died for them, and rose again. (II Corinthians 5:15)

And the scripture, foreseeing that God would justify the heathen through faith, preached before the gospel unto Abraham, saying, In thee shall **all** nations be blessed. (Galatians 3:8)

But the scripture hath concluded **all** under sin, that the promise by faith of Jesus Christ might be given to them that believe. (Galatians 3:22)

There is neither Jew nor Greek, there is neither bond nor free, there is neither male nor female: for ye are **all** one in Christ Jesus. (Galatians 3:28)

And to make **all** men see what is the fellowship of the mystery, which from the beginning of the world hath been hid in God, who created all things by Jesus Christ. (Ephesians 3:9)

One God and Father of all, who is above all, and through all, and in you **all**. But unto **every** one of us is given grace according to the measure of the gift of Christ. (Ephesians 4:6–7)

Till we **all** come in the unity of the faith, and of the knowledge of the Son of God, unto a perfect man, unto the measure of the stature of the fulness of Christ. (Ephesians 4:13)

In whom we have redemption through his blood, even the forgiveness of sins: Who is the image of the invisible God, the firstborn of **every** creature. (Colossians 1:14–15)

And, having made peace through the blood of his cross, by him to reconcile **all** things unto himself; by him, I say, whether they be things in earth, or things in heaven. (Colossians 1:20)

Whom we preach, warning **every** man, and teaching **every** man in all wisdom; that we may present **every** man perfect in Christ Jesus. (Colossians 1:28)

And you, being dead in your sins and the uncircumcision of your flesh, hath he quickened together with him, having forgiven you **all** trespasses. (Colossians 2:13)

Where there is neither Greek nor Jew, circumcision nor uncircumcision, Barbarian, Scythian, bond nor free: but Christ is all, and in **all**. (Colossians 3:11)

And the Lord make you to increase and abound in love one toward another, and toward **all** men, even as we do toward you. (I Thessalonians 3:12)

When he shall come to be glorified in his saints, and to be admired in **all** them that believe (because our testimony among you was believed) in that day. (II Thessalonians 1:10)

Howbeit for this cause I obtained mercy, that in me first Jesus Christ might shew forth all longsuffering, for a pattern to **them** which should hereafter believe on him to life everlasting. (I Timothy 1:16)

I exhort therefore, that, first of all, supplications, prayers, intercessions, and giving of thanks, be made for **all** men. (I Timothy 2:1)

Who will have **all** men to be saved, and to come unto the knowledge of the truth. (I Timothy 2:4)

Who gave himself a ransom for **all**, to be testified in due time. (I Timothy 2:6)

For therefore we both labour and suffer reproach, because we trust in the living God, who is the Saviour of **all** men, specially of those that believe. (I Timothy 4:10)

Henceforth there is laid up for me a crown of righteousness, which the Lord, the righteous judge, shall give me at that day: and not to me only, but unto **all** them also that love his appearing. (2 Timothy 4:8)

Notwithstanding the Lord stood with me, and strengthened me; that by me the preaching might be fully known, and that **all** the Gentiles might hear: and I was delivered out of the mouth of the lion. (2 Timothy 4:17)

For the grace of God that bringeth salvation hath appeared to **all** men. (Titus 2:11)

But we see Jesus, who was made a little lower than the angels for the suffering of death, crowned with glory and honour; that he by the grace of God should taste death for **every** man. (Hebrews 2:9)

The Lord is not slack concerning his promise, as some men count slackness; but is longsuffering to us-ward, not willing that **any** should perish, but that **all** should come to repentance. (2 Peter 3:9)

And he is the propitiation for our sins: and not for ours only, but for the sins of the **whole** world. (1 John 2:2)

And we have seen and do testify that the Father sent the Son to be the Saviour of the **world**. **Whosoever** shall confess that Jesus is the Son of God, God dwelleth in him, and he in God. (1 John 4:14–15)

Amen!

APPENDIX III

This quote was taken from the book: *Commentary on Ephesians* (pages 132–133) by Pastor Paul Sadler, D.D., Berean Bible Society, used with permission.

A Controversial Passage

"Whereby, when ye read, ye may understand my knowledge in the mystery of Christ) Which in other ages was not made known unto the sons of men, as it is now revealed unto his holy apostles and prophets by the Spirit" (Ephesians 3:4–5).

Those of the Acts 2 persuasion argue that the Mystery was made known to ages and generations past, but not as fully as it is now revealed to his apostles and prophets. In other words, Paul was not the first to receive it. They base this conclusion on Ephesians 3:5.

The proper exegesis of this passage hinges on the phrase "as it is now revealed." Therefore, we must determine whether the term "as" is used in the comparative or the contrastive sense. Perhaps an illustration will prove to be helpful: I might say: My golf game is as good as yours. Here the "as" is used in the comparative sense—I am comparing your game with mine. Turning to the contrastive side of our term we might say: The ancient Egyptians did not have computers as we do today. Applying our illustration to the passage in question we have two possibilities:

1. The Mystery was revealed prior to Paul, but not as (comparative) fully as it is today.
2. The Mystery was not revealed to ages and generations past as (contrastive) it is today through Paul's gospel.

The Acts 2 dispensationalists opt for number one. Those of us who have come to see Paul's distinctive ministry defend number two; thus, we have two opinions—but who is to say which one is correct? We are reminded at such times of the thought-provoking words of Elijah: "How long halt ye between two opinions?" (I Kings 18:21). The solution lies in the answer to the question, "What saith the Lord?" The following passages prove beyond a shadow of a doubt that the "as" is used in the contrastive sense in Ephesians 3:5, which can only mean the revelation of the Mystery was initially committed to Paul.

> Now to Him that is of power to establish you according to my (Paul's) gospel, and the preaching of Jesus Christ according to the revelation of the Mystery, which has been KEPT SECRET since the world began. (Romans 16:25)

> If you have heard of the dispensation of the grace of God which is given me (Paul) to youward: how that by revelation He made known unto me the Mystery... . And to make all men see what is the fellowship of the Mystery, which from the beginning of the world hath been HID in God, who created all things by Jesus Christ. (Ephesians 3:2, 9)

So then, while Paul received the Mystery by direct revelation from the Lord of glory, the apostles and prophets, and those since, have received it through the illumination of the Spirit (Galatians 1:11–12; cf. Ephesians 3:5). A knowledge of this glorious message is only obtainable through the enlightenment of the Holy Spirit. And it has been our experience that those who are in search of the key that unlocks the sacred secret are never denied access.

BIBLE INDEX

Bible Index

2:14-16	23
2:16	54
3:1-9	22
3:2	12, 17
3:2-6	66
3:2, 9	146
3:4-5	145
3:5	145, 146, 147
3:8-9	49
3:9	11, 17, 49, 104, 141
3:12	81
4:4-5	17
4:4-6	69, 94, 136
4:4-7	25
4:6-7	141
4:13	37, 141
4:14	37, 117
4:30	68, 121
4:32	67, 114
5:6	124
Philippians 1:23-24	122
2:8	82
3:9	82
3:20-21	85
Colossians 1:14	67
1:14-15	141
1:20	141
1:28	141
2:8	95, 112
2:10	34
2:10-15	88

155

About the Author:

During the forty-five-year pursuit, Fred was a professional in the financial services industry. He was active on many boards, organizations, and committees in his church and industry. He is a US Army Vietnam veteran, was married to his late wife, Jan, for fifty-seven years, and has three grown children and two grandchildren. Hobbies include family activities, traveling in a motor home, writing, speaking, oldies music, and muscle cars.

Contact Fred:
Email: fredlewis@biblicaladvancedbasics.com
Website: www.biblicaladvancedbasics.com

ORDER INFORMATION

To order additional copies of this book, please visit
www.redemption-press.com.
Also available on Amazon.com and BarnesandNoble.com
Or by calling toll free 1-844-2REDEEM.